Twenty-Eight Elephants and other Everyday Miracles

By Jacquie Gauthier

First published in 2017

Edited by Tracey Hawthorne
Cover by Sarah Currie
Photographs © Jacquie Gauthier,
except on p233, which is © Dianne Tipping-Woods

CreateSpace Independent Publishing Platform

ISBN 978-1-5484-6332-8

For Marita,
who has always believed in miracles,
and in me.

And for miraculous Michaela,
who always chooses joy.

What is it about Africa?

I've been asked that question many times and I struggle to
find the words to describe this incredible place.

For me, it's exciting and exotic like nowhere else on earth, but
from the moment I arrived, I felt like I'd come home.
Africa is, literally, the cradle of mankind,
where we all had our beginnings.
Even when you come to Africa for the first time you have,
in a sense, returned.

There's a beauty and simplicity to life here.
There's also complication and harshness.
Maybe the magic lies in the contrast.

"... fortune holds some gifts in store for those who try ..."
— *Percy FitzPatrick,* Jock of the Bushveld

"If I have ever seen magic, it has been in Africa."
— *John Hemingway, American author*

"I never knew of a morning in Africa when I woke up
that I was not happy."
— *Ernest Hemingway, American author and journalist*

Foreword

In 2015, when Jacquie Gauthier was writing *The Gift of an Elephant*, we met online through an introduction by a mutual friend. Jacquie was interested in learning more about publishing her book and I was happy to share my experience. She went on to launch her delightful memoir in the autumn of 2015 and we met in person then, as she promoted the book in Canada.

Our connection as friends and writers has grown from that first meeting. It's something I value tremendously.

In *The Gift of an Elephant*, Jacquie took us along on her surprising journey, which in many ways was a coming of age in midlife. We followed her from her decades as a popular radio morning-show host in London, Ontario to her life-changing volunteer mission in South Sudan, where a whirlwind romance led to an email courtship, an elopement and a new beginning in South Africa.

When the book ended, Jacquie wondered — as did we — just where this journey would take her.

As you're about to find out in this, the second instalment of her memoir, it's been quite a ride! And it's our privilege to follow along as Jacquie finds her place in the unique experience that is life in Africa.

She candidly shares her intimate personal emotional transformations. We applaud as her photographic and creative artistic talents lead her into a life of wildlife conservation and local education. She brings us smiles and tears as she touchingly paints pictures of what it means to embrace life in her new world.

I love Jacquie's story for a long list of reasons, but mainly because she took a chance with life.

We never know what fate will hand us from one day to the next. Every day is a gift, and through her memoirs, Jacquie touches our hearts and reminds us to never give up.

She is a true possibilitarian!

Patricia Sands
Award-winning author of the *Love in Provence* series, June 2017

Prologue

Life is always calling you forward.

You may not feel ready, you may think you don't want to go, but suddenly circumstances change and you're forced to take a different direction — perhaps one you'd never even considered before. It's life's way of helping you expand, and while it often doesn't feel like it at the time, it's almost always a good thing.

When this change of direction happens, some of the people in your life will go on the journey with you. Others, uncomfortable with your evolution, may leave your life abruptly or just slowly drift away. You may feel hurt and abandoned at the time but know that it's okay — you just don't fit together any more. Find comfort in the knowledge that new beginnings are born from painful endings.

I know this from experience. Life had been calling me forward for quite some time, but I'd refused to budge. It had seemed as if there was too much to risk. I was well into my forties and I had a great job as a media personality. I was married and I had my little dream home. I should've been happy, and I often told myself that I was. Wanting more seemed selfish, so I kept trying to convince myself that "this is as good as it gets".

But life kept whispering that there was something more. I could hear the call but I was too afraid to heed it. In time, the whisper evolved into a tap on the shoulder. I stubbornly ignored it for fear of losing everything I'd worked so hard to accomplish. I was middle-aged, for crying out loud! Surely it was too late to change my life?

Eventually came the bricks to the head that couldn't be ignored. In quick succession my marriage ended, my campaign for Canadian parliament failed and I lost my high-profile job as a radio morning-show host. Some of the people I loved and had thought would be with me forever vanished from my life. There was nothing left to cling to. I had no choice but to move on. As described in my book *The Gift of an Elephant*, the choice was somewhat thrust upon me...

Taking the opportunity of this unasked-for hiatus in my life, I fulfilled a long-held dream of going on an aid trip to South Sudan. As part of a team from Canadian Aid for South Sudan, I helped put on a daily art-and-music camp for children in the village of Gordhim. We also made a side trip up to the Darfur border to deliver medicine to a refugee camp. The experiences I had in those few weeks would have been life changing on their own but then something completely unexpected happened: I met the love of my life.

After a six-month email courtship, we eloped and moved to my husband's home country of South Africa, where we rented a tiny cottage outside the small town of Hoedspruit, on the edge of the Kruger National Park in Limpopo province. The transition wasn't easy, but it was exciting, challenging and, above all, enlightening.

Now here we are, two years later.

Are we settled? Far from it!

As I write this, we're nearly four years into our marriage and on the surface it would appear that not much has changed. Johann continues his contract job as a paramedic in Mozambique, so we're still apart six months out of every twelve. He has no job security, and I'm still at least two years away from being legally allowed to work in South Africa. I miss my family and friends.

Yet despite all this, I'm happier and more optimistic than I've ever been. How can that be?

I've changed.

The old me would've demanded that conditions change in order for me to be happy. I would've needed Johann to have a secure job and a growing bank account, and to be at home every night. I would've needed to be able to go home at least a couple of times a year to visit my family and friends. Those would've been my minimum requirements for happiness.

But since taking the huge leap of faith and moving to South Africa, I've started to see things differently.

I'm learning to live unconditionally.

It occurred to me a few years ago that I, and pretty much everyone else I know, live life from the outside in. We start by observing external conditions: the circumstances we experience and the behaviour of the people around us. We then make a judgment about those circumstances and that behaviour. If they're "good", we're happy. If they're "bad", we're unhappy. In this way, we allow existing conditions to determine how we feel.

I think we have it backwards. Through my own life experience, it's become clear to me that the key is to live from the inside out: to choose to be happy, and then watch the circumstances — and other people — line up with that.

Happiness is indeed a choice, and one that we can make any time. Every moment is a new opportunity to choose.

What better time to choose happiness than now?

Chapter 1

Outside of Hoedspruit, South Africa, January 2013. It was 5am, and I awoke to the sound of my neighbour's angry voice. This was my new and very disturbing alarm clock, five days a week. On the weekends I got a small reprieve: the shouting usually didn't start until around 6am.

Things had changed dramatically in our idyllic little world at the foot of the Drakensberg. Our tranquil spot in the valley had become nothing short of chaotic since our benevolent landlords had decided to sell the property and move into a small place in a nearby town. The new owners had a completely different vision for Ver End Lodge. It was their retirement plan and, understandably, they wanted to make their investment pay.

They began adding more structures to the property, including a small tuckshop and the beginnings of a caravan park. In came more people, and with them more vehicles and several barking dogs. The colourful kingfishers, purple louries and paradise flycatchers I'd so loved to watch in our birdbath had become scarce, probably because of all the activity and noise. Fences went up around the perimeter of the property, barring the impala and nyala antelope from wandering through the garden.

I was missing my furry and feathered friends and the joy they'd brought me every day.

Soon there was talk of placing security cameras in a few strategic locations around the property. Why, I wasn't sure. My husband Johann and I had felt very safe living here these last two years. I never worried even when he was away for a month at a time, working as a medic in Mozambique, and I was on my own. In the fifteen years of the lodge's existence there'd never been a break-in — until they put up the fence. I couldn't help but wonder if putting up the fence had given people the idea that there were things of value worth stealing on the other side.

Our old neighbours, Oom and Tannie, had moved away several months before. We'd been sad to see them go, but delighted that we were offered the chance to move into their cottage. It was much nicer than the one we'd taken, sight unseen, when we'd moved to Hoedspruit two years before. I was thrilled to have a full-sized kitchen, with a countertop larger than a cutting board and plenty of cupboards for storage. This cottage also came equipped with a full-sized stove and oven — a huge relief after trying to prepare meals on a two-plate cooker. Yes, we were definitely moving up in the world!

The building we now inhabited had originally been a large three-bedroom cottage. A wall had been erected, dividing the space into two very uneven sections. We lived in the front, which had become a charming two-bedroom flat. On the other side of the bedroom walls was a cramped bachelor flat. The space was small for even one person to live in, so we were shocked when the new tenants arrived: a family of four!

Shortly after they moved in, Johann had to return to Mozambique, where his then paramedic contract had him running the clinic on a railway-restoration project. I should've been used to the one-month-together/one-month-apart nature of our marriage by then, but I still always found it difficult to say goodbye to my husband when he left for his thirty-day rotation. And now I wouldn't even have the company of our old landlords or our friendly former neighbours.

It didn't take long to see that the chances of my striking up a friendship with the man next door were slim to none. He was under a lot of pressure. He had custody of his three young children, and was stretched to the limit emotionally and financially. The tiny flat was all he could afford and it was obvious that the confined quarters were making matters worse. His angry voice was the first thing I heard in the morning and the last thing I heard as I tried to drift off to sleep at night.

After a few weeks it became obvious that something had to give.

I decided I'd try to pick the right moment and speak with him when things were relatively calm. After about a week I wondered if that moment would ever come, but eventually the perfect opportunity presented itself.

The morning had started off bright and ugly, with the usual sounds of chaos coming from next door. It was always such a relief to hear the distinctive sound of the old Volkswagen Beetle's engine as he started it up and they set off for work and school. I made myself a cup of rooibos tea and settled in on the porch with my laptop to write a few emails.

About an hour later I was surprised to hear the VW making its way back down the driveway. As he parked the car, I got up and walked towards him. He tensed visibly as I approached.

"Everything okay?" I asked.

"Aren't you going to yell at me?" he challenged. "Everyone else has."

"Hadn't planned on it," I replied.

His stance relaxed. "Good. I can't handle any more trouble this morning. My son forgot his homework and now I've had to come all the way back here and waste my petrol. It costs so much to go back and forth into town, but this is the only place I can afford. And everyone here is complaining about us and wants us gone."

As much as I wasn't enjoying having him as a neighbour, I couldn't help but feel for him. "You must be so tired," I said.

The comment took him by surprise. The glare in his eyes softened, showing a glimpse of the person behind the anger. "I am," he said. "It's so easy for people to judge. I'm doing my best."

Now that his defences were down, his story poured out. His wife had left him and was now pregnant with another man's child. They lived close by, and he struggled with the hurt and humiliation of the situation whenever he saw them.

I listened, nodding in understanding of his plight. It was obviously a relief for him to be able to talk to someone.

"Anyway, I have to get going," he said. "I have to get back to the school, and then I'll be late for work. Sorry we're so loud. I'll try to do better. Thanks for talking to me."

"I think we'll all cope better if we get more sleep," I said, and added, "and if you'd like to talk again, I'd be happy to listen."

I went back to my chair on the porch while he went inside to collect the forgotten homework. Soon he was back in his little Volkswagen for the 27-kilometre trip into town.

As I watched him drive away, I thought about our interaction and felt truly pleased with the way it had unfolded. I'd consciously been trying to change an old behaviour that didn't serve me, and it appeared I was succeeding.

At some stage in my childhood I'd decided that the way to be liked was to be needed. I became what psychologists term a "rescuer". Had I been looking for a pattern, I would've seen evidence of it in every romantic relationship I'd ever had, but I wasn't that self-aware. I'd had no idea that I was a textbook case of a personality type; I'd just thought I wanted to help.

And the compulsion wasn't limited to just romantic relationships; I'd do pretty much anything to help anyone. If there was a problem, I'd rush in and fix it — no one would even have to ask. And if you were someone I loved, well, there seemed to be no limit to what I'd do for you.

In my mind I was being noble and coming from a position of strength but over the years I'd finally come to understand that it was neither. My behaviour enabled the other person's helplessness and fed my need to be needed. That left one of us disempowered and the other insecure – and exhausted.

Now, it really pleased me to know that I was changing my behaviour. When I'd spoken to my neighbour I'd been kind and empathetic, but I hadn't taken on his problems and gotten myself involved.

My new awareness had been cemented after a recent situation I hadn't handled nearly as well.

Shortly after we moved to Hoedspruit I'd had made the acquaintance of a beautiful, charismatic woman from Europe. We

22

became fast friends. Her story was compelling and certainly struck a chord with me; she too had ended up in South Africa as the result of a whirlwind romance, and was now living blissfully in the bush with her beloved.

At least, that was the version she told. It wasn't long before the cracks in that fractured fairytale began to show and she divulged that the man was abusive, and that she was living in fear. From the start it had been a tumultuous affair, and this time when he left she decided to change the locks.

Of course, that was my cue. She seemed devastated and helpless, qualities this "rescuer" just couldn't resist. While Johann was away working in Mozambique, I stayed with her for a few weeks, helping her to pick up the emotional pieces while packing up his things. She planned to put his belongings in a storage locker for him to collect, thus avoiding any further contact or conflict.

After being with her for a few days, I really wondered what I had gotten myself into. She told me that he carried a gun, and when I was packing up I found the bullets that seemed to prove it. As I lay wide awake in bed that night, jumping at every little sound, I wondered if we were in real physical danger. I talked to Johann about it the next time we were able to connect. He too was worried, and suggested that she move in with me instead of my staying with her, so that if her former partner did decide to show up at her place, he'd find an empty house.

The point became moot, however, when, inexplicably, she took her abuser back.

Once he'd regained his status in the house, he easily convinced her that I was the reason for the rupture in their relationship. Suddenly I was persona non grata. She was told never to speak to me again and she meekly complied. If I sent her an email, he would answer. I was told in no uncertain terms that I was no longer part of her world. I was devastated at the loss of my friend and I worried for her safety.

As the months went on, I became angry — with myself. Although I hadn't known this woman well, I'd empathized with her completely. I'd made her problems my own, to the point of actually putting myself in possible physical danger.

Looking back on it, I could see the folly in my behaviour. When someone decides to walk along the railway tracks, you can walk beside them and warn them about the approaching train, but there's no reason to stand on the tracks with them as the speeding locomotive approaches. It's good to be kind and empathetic, but not at the cost of your own wellbeing. Now, after my talk with our tired, stressed new neighbour, I knew that I was making progress in getting out of the rescue business.

I'd hoped that after our little conversation the situation at Ver End would improve, but as the weeks passed it became clear that the only thing that had changed was my attitude. It was definitely time for us to move.

I told Johann of my plan the next time he called. "I think you're right, love. The time has come," he said. "But where will we move to? I'm not sure we can afford to rent a place in town."

"I'm sure we'll find something," I said, trying to feel optimistic but knowing that affordable rentals in Hoedspruit were as rare as pangolin sightings. Still, I'd already managed to see that elusive, endangered armadillo-type animal twice in the time I'd lived in the area. By comparison, finding an affordable place to live should have been easy.

It wasn't. A google search showed that the price of a flat in town would be at least double what we were paying for our little place by the mountain — and our current rent actually included water and electricity. On top of that, there weren't many options to choose from — but there was one that caught my eye. It was part of a complex called Raptors' Lodge, a collection of charming thatched-roofed two-bedroom units that were normally used as holiday rentals. The property was right in town, in walking distance of many shops and restaurants. Even so, it retained the feeling of being in the bush, with an abundance of birds and small animals like mongooses and porcupines making themselves at home.

It was perfect, but of course way out of our price range. I knew we couldn't afford it, but I couldn't stop thinking about it. Just out of curiosity, I sent a message to the rental agent asking for more details. My email went unanswered.

A few more days of futile searching for an affordable place convinced me that somehow we'd find a way to afford the unit in Raptors' Lodge. I sent another email to the rental agent, asking if by chance the expensive rental might include electricity.

This time she did reply, but only to say that in fact the price did not include electricity but that it was irrelevant anyway, as the unit had been rented out. I felt completely deflated.

Still, as the days went by, I couldn't get the idea of living at Raptors' Lodge out of my head. I did an internet search to see if there was another, hopefully more helpful estate agent who handled the units. There was. Her name was Joan, and I sent her a message asking if she would please keep us In mind should another unit come up for rent.

She responded immediately, asking if perhaps we might be in the market to buy. She knew one of the owners wanted to sell in a hurry, and was asking well below the going price of the other units that were currently listed. Would we like to come and have a look?

Before thinking it through, I shot back an email saying yes, we'd love to see it as soon as Johann returned from Mozambique. An appointment was set for later that week.

Could we actually do this? I wondered. It certainly wasn't something we'd been considering. For the past few years our financial situation had been precarious, to say the least. Johann's previous marriage had left him with a mountain of debt, and I'd used up most of my savings trying to keep the creditors at bay, and travelling back and forth to Canada.

But things were getting better now that he was working this contract in Mozambique. And I had a little bit of money stashed away from the sale of my house in Canada. Before I moved to South Africa, I'd handed it over to my friend and financial planner with strict instructions not to lose a cent of it. I'd been clinging to that bit of security like a life raft, never sure where we'd end up or what might happen along the way.

Now Hoedspruit was starting to feel like home. We'd already made some good friends here. Maybe it was time to release my grip on the life raft, relax and see if we could float.

I started to get very excited at the prospect of laying down roots in this patch of red African soil. I anxiously awaited Johann's return home so we could go and see the house.

It was a two-day odyssey for Johann to get from northern Mozambique back home to Hoedspruit. He'd leave the camp and catch the train in Cuamba. If he was lucky, his departure day would coincide with a day when they added a first-class car onto the train. That only happened twice a week, so the odds weren't in his favour. First class meant that instead of a hard bench, he got a decent seat, with a back that reclined a little and even a foot rest. More importantly, it also meant that he didn't have to travel with the chickens, goats and other assorted livestock on board.

On this particular trip, he was in luck — first class all the way to Nampula! It was only a 300-kilometre trip but it took thirteen hot and dusty hours because the train stopped in every little village along the way. At each stop, people got off and on, and livestock and other goods were loaded and offloaded. The train was the lifeline between all these small communities.

Once he arrived in Nampula, he'd walk the fifteen minutes to the hotel where he'd spend the night, then catch a plane the next day. The first leg of the flight was from Nampula to Maputo. That took two hours. Then he'd fly from Maputo to Johannesburg, another hour and a half. Once he landed in Jozi, he'd pick up a rental car and drive the five hours home to Hoedspruit. It was always close to midnight by the time he arrived.

As always, I greeted him at the door, literally jumping into his arms. He was exhausted and we went to bed almost immediately. He fell asleep as soon as his head hit the pillow, but I hardly slept that night. I was so excited! My husband was home and in the morning we were going to look at a house that we might actually be able to buy!

Early the next morning we drove into town to meet Joan at her office.

We entered the premises of Kruger 2 Canyon properties to find a petite, energetic woman who appeared to be in her late fifties sitting at a desk. After the introductions, we got straight down to business. She wanted to know more about our needs and our budget before showing us the unit for sale at Raptors' Lodge.

With our limited funds, it really did seem like a good fit. With a motivated seller asking less than market value, and with all the furniture, crockery, cutlery and even the linens included, it appeared to be the perfect choice for us.

We left the office and climbed into Joan's SUV for the two-minute drive to Safari Junction, a cul-de-sac that housed a restaurant, a wine bar, a spa and our potential new home. I knew I was going to like the neighbourhood!

Joan entered the code to the security gate and it slid open, allowing us through. This was something I still had to get used to. I grew up in a small town in Canada where most properties weren't fenced, and many people didn't even bother to lock their doors. Mind you, they didn't have transient leopards and lions or destructive baboons to consider...

From the outside, the unit looked just like the pictures I'd seen online, with a quaint garden in the front and a paving-stone path leading to a small thatched bungalow. Based on all the reasons that made it a perfect solution for us, I'd utterly convinced myself that I'd absolutely love the place.

Joan put the key in the lock and the door swung open. We stepped inside and it took a moment for our eyes to adjust from the bright sunlight outside.

I didn't love it. Not at all. Neither did Johann.

The living room was small and dark and crammed with furniture. The walls were nicotine yellow, while the fireplace was painted a sickly shade of terracotta orange.

The kitchen was part of this main room, with a small counter housing the stove and a cooktop. The counter served as the only divider between the two spaces. The kitchen space was so tiny that if you were standing at the stove, you literally just had to turn around to be standing at the single sink, next to which there was another tiny counter.

These units, designed as holiday rentals, might have served their purpose as temporary accommodation but it looked as if they'd prove awkward and challenging for everyday life.

Sensing our disappointment, Joan quickly ushered us into the master bedroom — and we were completely wowed by the big, bright, beautiful space. The centrepiece of the room was a king-size bed romantically draped in mosquito netting. It immediately brought to mind the luxury safari tent Johann and I had stayed in when we'd eloped. And this bedroom included a spacious en-suite and an outdoor shower — something that had been high on both our wish lists.

We looked at each other, beaming. There was precious little closet space, but that seemed a minor consideration, and it was obvious that we were both thinking that surely there must be some way we could improve the kitchen/living-room area...

Joan then opened the bedroom's sliding doors with a flourish, and ushered us through to the back patio. The space was generous and surrounded by greenery. Birds chirped happily as they flitted from tree to tree.

And then we saw it — Johann's holy grail: a big outdoor fireplace equipped with a grill. His smile morphed into a huge grin. The property was as good as sold.

"I can see you're very excited about this but I'm not sure you should put in an offer on the first place you see," Joan said, sensibly. "Let me do a bit of research and I'll find a few others for you to look at."

We had to agree that that would be the rational thing to do, so we planned to meet again later in the week when she'd lined up a few more properties for us to see.

Later that evening I was checking my emails, and I decided to flip over to Facebook to see what was new. A post on the Hoedspruit Town page immediately caught my eye. It was a casting call for the American TV show *House Hunters International*. For an upcoming episode, they were looking for foreigners who were interested in buying a house in South Africa.

I'd seen the show once before, and I knew that part of the deal was a return trip to your home country to show the contrast between your previous life and the new one you were about to embark on. I clicked on the link and applied immediately. A free trip to Canada was all the incentive I needed. I wasn't so sure about my shy, private husband, though — would he be willing to perform for the camera? I decided to see if the show would even consider us before I broached the subject with Johann.

The answer came back within a day. Yes, they'd love to interview us because our story sounded so interesting. I asked Johann how he felt about being on international television and was pleasantly surprised by his response. "It'll be a very different experience for me," he observed, "but that seems to be what life with you is all about."

We did a Skype interview with the producer, and on the strength of that, the selection process came down to us and one other couple. We were then asked to submit a video of the two of us giving a tour of one of the prospective houses. Ultimately, the producers liked both stories so much that they decided to do both, but we didn't find that out until much later.

A date was set for the four-day shoot, and I sent the producer a list of suggested locations for filming to best showcase our new home town. It was a great opportunity to highlight so many of the people and places I'd come to know and love in and around Hoedspruit.

With us still being relatively new to the area and the crew coming from different locations in the world — the director was Australian, the cameraman from England and the sound guy from Johannesburg — it was important to have someone with good local knowledge on the shoot. And they found the ideal person for the job. Tracy had been the on-camera real-estate agent in an earlier episode of the show they'd filmed in Hoedspruit a few years before, and when the producers contacted her asking whom they might hire as a production assistant this time round, she decided to take the job herself.

Tracy's can-do attitude coupled with her large social and business network made her the perfect appointee. She could source anything in short order, from potted plants to late-night snacks. She was also clever, charming and wickedly funny, which helped boost lagging spirits as the hours of filming crept into the double digits each day. Before the end of day one, I knew I'd found a kindred spirit.

Johann and I had a great time showing the television crew our new world. We visited Nyani Cultural Village, a replica of a traditional Shangaan tribal village where the local culture is brought to life by incredibly gifted singers, dancers and drummers. Next, we were off to Camp Jabulani, a lodge that was created to give a home to a group of orphaned elephants. The crew loved their up-close elephant experience — with the possible exception of Kevin, the sound guy, who had to keep dodging elephant droppings as he followed along behind the herd, trying to record our dialogue.

I also got to take the crew to the place nearest and dearest to my heart, Tanda Tula safari camp. I'd started volunteer-teaching adult literacy and English to the staff at the camp shortly after we moved to Hoedspruit, and I loved everything about it. The hour-long trip out to the property was like a game drive, and teaching the amazing staff was one of the most fulfilling things I'd ever done.

I also had the incredible privilege of going out on game drives with some of the best guides and trackers in southern Africa. Guides Formen and Scotch were always eager to share their extensive knowledge and enthusiasm with me, and we'd become good friends. Likewise, master tracker Jack had a soft spot in his heart for me, taking every opportunity to try to teach me to read tracks and signs, and never showing any signs of frustration when I consistently proved to be completely inept at the art. Trackers Patrick and Jeffrey were also on board to coach me, their smiles and patience never waning as I tried to guess what had made the marks they would point out to me in the sand. Every game drive was an adventure, and my days at Tanda Tula were among the happiest of my life.

It was fun having the *House Hunters* crew there, and they got great footage of me teaching a class, with Scotch in particular really enjoying his fifteen minutes of fame.

Overall, the experience of being on the *House Hunters* show was wonderful but it was exhausting. The show is shot with minimal crew: a director, a sound technician and a cameraman.

Because there's only one camera, every scene has to be shot several times, each time with the camera in a different position to give the editor varied footage to work with. This was the most challenging part — doing the same scene over and over, trying to remember how we'd moved and what we'd said. Johann decided soon into the process that a career in television was not something he aspired to.

The four days of March filming wrapped in hot-as-Hades Hoedspruit, and it was time to leave for Canada.

According to the calendar, spring officially arrives in the northern hemisphere on 21 March. It was early April when we landed in London, Ontario, the city where I'd spent twenty years of my thirty-year radio career. We'd expected to see green buds on the trees and to find the crocuses and daffodils blooming but the leaves and flowers evidently knew better and had remained dormant. The biting cold and howling wind made it clear winter wasn't quite ready to leave just yet. I marvelled at how quickly I'd acclimatized to the heat of South Africa and wondered if I'd ever be able to cope with a Canadian winter again!

We made our way to my friend Lynn's house, which now served as our home base in London. She'd also generously allowed the TV crew to film there because my old house had, of course, long since been sold.

We settled in and checked the call sheet the production company had sent with the details and schedule for the shoot the next day. It indicated that we'd be doing several scenes outdoors, and that the day would start early. We hoped for sunshine and light winds.

The sun played along, but the stubborn wind wouldn't let up. Once the wind-chill factor was taken into account, if felt as if the temperature was well below freezing.

We were learning a lot about "reality television", which I think should be called "reality-*inspired* television" — a far more accurate name. We were about to recreate some events in my life that had happened years before; and, more interestingly, we were going to stage an event that I only wished had happened. Ah, the magic of television!

The crew arrived at Lynn's house and scouted the premises to determine where we'd sit for the interview segment. It was a different crew this time, as for each location the show puts out a call to the various professionals they use, and then hires whoever is closest and available. Eventually, the new director determined the best angle for the shot, and Johann and I were perched awkwardly on a piano stool. We were uncomfortable before the tape started to roll, and it only got worse.

The camera's red light flashed and the questions started, first directed at me.

"How does it feel leaving behind everything familiar?"

"You seem to have a lot of friends and are close with your family. Aren't you afraid of being so far away and isolated?"

"You had a big career, and now you're going somewhere you can't legally work. How will you cope?"

"What is it about this man that makes you willing to give up everything and move to the other side of the world?"

Although I'd already been living my new life in Africa for almost three years, the questions hit me hard. I had no regrets, but I once again realized the enormity of the changes I'd made in the name of love. I responded as best I could while trying to stop the tears from spilling out with the answers. The intensity of the emotion caught me completely by surprise.

Eventually the interviewer shifted her focus to Johann.

"Do you worry that your wife will be alone so much of the time?"

"How do you think she'll cope with missing you and all her friends and family?"

"It's not home for you either, and you'll be away half the time. How will you be able to make it feel like home?"

By the time the interviews finished a few hours later, we both felt like we'd been put through the emotional wringer. And it was only 9am — we still had ten hours of filming ahead of us!

The crew packed up the equipment and took off ahead of us to set up at the next location — the radio station where I'd worked with my on-air partner for nearly twenty years; the same radio station that had "downsized" me three years before. I hadn't been back since the day I was escorted from the building after being told that the show I'd just finished was my last. I was already feeling emotionally raw, and I worried how I'd react when I walked through those doors again.

Luckily, I didn't have to do it alone. As we pulled into the parking lot, I saw my erstwhile on-air partner, Dave, waiting at the door. He jokingly referred to himself as being bulletproof, having survived several more rounds of brutal job cuts at the radio station after I'd been let go.

Dave gave me a big hug, and he and Johann shook hands. I think that both my old friend and I sensed that this was an opportunity to finally have closure on the long career we'd had together. Although we'd seen each other personally since I'd lost my job, we'd never had the chance to say a professional goodbye. I'd been there one day and gone the next.

Ours was an unlikely friendship because Dave and I were complete opposites, but we'd been through so much during the time of our on-air partnership that we'd formed a strong bond. I used to joke that our partnership was just like a bad marriage: we'd been together for years, fought all the time and didn't have sex.

Dave and I had seen each other through many ups and downs. When we first started working together, I was single and he was married. Then his marriage ended, and I got married. Later I got divorced, and he remarried. It seemed now we'd both found our happiness, he with his new wife and their young daughter, and me with my wonderful husband and a new life in South Africa.

We all walked into the building and made our way down the corridor to the studio that had been the home of our morning show for so many years. It was all so familiar, but nothing was the same. I didn't recognize any of the performers on the new posters on the wall. I saw my old chair, but there was a different set of headphones looped over its arm: they belonged to Dave's new on-air partner.

We chatted for a few minutes while the cameraman went outside to set up. Then I left Johann and Dave in the warm studio and headed back out into the bitter cold.

I was given instructions to get into the car and drive away from the building, then turn around and come back as if I were just arriving. The cameraman, Mike, filmed me pulling into the lot, parking, and getting out of my car and going into the radio station, just as I'd done each weekday morning for so many years.

We moved inside and the camera followed me walking down the corridor and into the studio. Mike then moved into the studio and positioned the camera to capture my entrance.

As I stood outside the door, waiting for my cue to walk in, I got butterflies in my stomach. This was it: the opportunity I thought I'd never have; a chance for me to say goodbye to Dave and to the loyal audience who'd listened to us for nearly two decades. And even though we were faking the whole scene for the benefit of the camera, the tears at the end for both of us were real.

By the time filming wrapped around 8pm, Johann and I had relived a few more of the gut-wrenching episodes we'd experienced on our real-life journey. We'd re-enacted saying goodbye at the airport when Johann was leaving Canada to start his job in Mozambique and we didn't know when I'd be able to follow. We shot that scene half a dozen times, and each take hit me harder. Johann tried to lighten things up, joking that the people inside the airport must have thought he was nuts — kissing me goodbye, then walking through the revolving door, only to come straight back out and do it all again. And again.

By the time we got to the last scene of the day, I was an emotional wreck. We'd staged a farewell dinner with Lynn at a downtown restaurant, and I was on the verge of tears from the moment we sat down.

The director finally decided to call it a day because I couldn't keep it together any more. My reaction was so ridiculous that even I had to laugh through my tears. The reality was that the move had been made, and I was happy in Africa. And I wasn't saying goodbye to my dear friends just yet — I still had a few weeks left in Canada.

But doing the show had given me a deeper realisation of just how profoundly my world had changed. There was no turning back, and in fact we were about to take a big leap forward: we got the news that our purchase offer on the unit at Raptors' Lodge had been accepted.

I was very excited at the prospect of us owning our own home, and was anxious to make the purchase, but of course it was going to be a bit complicated. The cash had to be transferred from Canada to the lawyer's account in South Africa. The transfer seemed to go smoothly from the Canadian side, but the money failed to show up on the South African end. For several nerve-wracking days, the money didn't appear, seemingly lost somewhere in cyberspace. And all the while the exchange rate of the South African rand to the Canadian dollar kept dropping — not in our favour! I worried that the deal might fall through before the cash came in, but it finally appeared in the lawyer's account.

From there, things proceeded in the normal South African way, which for me was far from normal. I was dismayed to discover that the business of property transfer in South Africa was completely different to the system in Canada. I was accustomed to putting in a bid on a property, agreeing on a closing date, and having the property transfer on that day. It was all pretty simple and efficient. You knew what day you were moving, so you could give notice on a rental or coordinate your closing date with the buyer of your home if you were selling a property. You could also book movers.

In South Africa, there was no closing date. Once your offer was accepted, you paid the money and waited for the transfer to go through. It could take a few weeks or a few months. It made no sense to me that we couldn't plan our move.

We gave notice to the owners of our little cottage and hoped that the timing would work out.

Johann and I during the filming of House Hunters International *in South Africa*

Filming of House Hunters International *in Canada*

Dave and I

Lynn, our "home base" in London, Canada

Chapter 2

I love it when a plan comes together.

We were back home in Hoedspruit, and on the last day before Johann had to head back to Mozambique, which just happened to coincide with the end of the month, we got the okay to move into our new place. We'd packed up everything that week and had the trailer loaded, anticipating that somehow the timing would be just right and it would all work out.

It took a few trips back and forth, but we got the last of the boxes unloaded into our new home in time for Johann to have a few hours' sleep and then start the long drive back down to Jozi to catch his flight. I'd have plenty of time to get things sorted out while he was gone.

I saw him off at 4am, and decided to go back to bed for a while. It was still pitch dark and I was tired. Just as I started to drift off to sleep, I heard a scuffling noise coming from the kitchen.

I sat bolt upright in bed, frantically searching for the bedside lamp. With the bedroom light on, I peered into the living room, but it was still too dark for my liking.

I found my torch and shone it around the living room and kitchen areas. I couldn't see anything, and the noise had stopped.

I ventured into the kitchen and turned on the light. The silence continued, and I wondered if it had been a dream.

I went back to the bedroom and climbed back into bed. I was just about to switch off the light when I heard the noise again.

I ran back into the kitchen. and waited. When I heard it again, I realized the noise was the sound of claws scratching on the ceiling right above my head. Something was living in the small attic — but what?

I raced back into the bedroom, closing the door behind me. I sat on the bed, clutching at my chest to slow down my racing heart.

My fear was soon replaced by embarrassment, however. This was exactly how I didn't want to react to these kinds of situations. I'd taken a nature-guide course which included spending three weeks in the bush learning about all the animals I might encounter. I'd spent time at Khamai Reptile Park with the local reptile experts, learning about snakes and lizards. I'd been so proud of myself, the girl who was terrified of spiders and snakes, who had willingly allowed a big hairy baboon spider to walk across the palm of her hand, and who'd posed for a photo with an enormous cobra wrapped around her neck. I was actually starting to understand these creatures and appreciate their beauty, so why was I freaking out because one of them was living in the attic?

As I calmed down, I realized that I really should've expected it. I'd bought a home in wildlife territory — of course any creature would seek shelter in a protected, dry space like the one between my kitchen ceiling and the thatched roof! The fact that my name was on the title deed was of no importance to the current occupants. I'd have to learn to live with them.

I went back into the kitchen and listened some more, trying to work out what the creature might be. It couldn't be a snake because it wasn't a slithering sound, it was a scratching sound. Maybe it was just a squirrel? No, it was definitely much bigger than a squirrel. Perhaps a mongoose? No, it was moving too slowly. A lizard seemed the most likely candidate. A really big lizard.

Although I was feeling much calmer, I wasn't feeling brave enough to climb up onto the counter and open the trapdoor in the ceiling to confirm my theory. I decided to bring in reinforcements for that, but it would have to wait a few hours until Calvin and Magic arrived for work. The two were charged with looking after the gardens and doing outdoor maintenance at Raptors' Lodge. I hoped their job descriptions included reptile relocation.

I knew there was no way I'd get back to sleep, so I started to unpack boxes while I waited for their arrival.

At 7am sharp I met Calvin and Magic at the gate, and tried to explain my situation. Luckily their English was a little better than my pathetic Tsonga. They conferred quickly, grabbed a ladder from the tool shed and went to my unit to investigate. In the kitchen, Calvin asked for my torch, then climbed up the ladder and pushed open the small trapdoor. The upper part of his body disappeared by degrees as he climbed the rungs, until we could only see him from the knees down.

There was silence, then his muffled voice came from above: "Oh! She's big!"

Magic and I looked at each other with eyes as wide as saucers.

Calvin scampered down the ladder, and quickly slid the trapdoor back into place before repeating his initial assessment. "She's big!" he exclaimed, adding, "Too big!"

Without another word, he strode out the door, Magic close on his heels. I stood there for a moment, not knowing what to do, then I raced out the door after them. "Does that mean you won't help me?" I called out in despair.

Calvin stopped and turned to face me. "One moment, madam," he said, holding up his hand in a gesture I took to mean "stay calm".

He and Magic then disappeared into the small tool shed. I stood outside and waited. They rifled around in there and emerged a few minutes later with a large broom and a caulking gun. I surmised the plan was to chase the creature out of the roof, then seal up any potential points of re-entry.

We went back into the house, Calvin confidently leading the charge. He quickly went back up the ladder, with Magic right behind. I could hear the creature scuffling across the ceiling as they chased it with the broom. I went outside in time to see a metre-long monitor lizard race out of the roof and clamber down the wall. It disappeared into the bush.

Soon the two men descended.

"She's gone," Calvin said simply.

"Thank you so much for your help!" I said with great sincerity and relief.

"No problem," he said, and carrying the ladder, they walked out the door. I made a mental note to give them both a big bonus the next month.

The rest of the day was uneventful by comparison. I unpacked boxes and sorted through all our newly acquired possessions. How lucky we were to have found a place that came equipped with everything! We now had beautiful modern white china and stainless-steel cutlery, and bedding and towels far nicer than those we'd been using at Ver End. Yes, the place was small, but with a coat of fresh paint to brighten it up, I was sure it would look and feel more spacious. The house wasn't perfect, but it was perfect for us. I went to bed feeling quite content.

As I was about to drift off to sleep, I heard the scuffling noise again. "She" was back!

This time, I didn't panic. Of course the lizard would come back. It was also content with this home, and wasn't about to be forced out. I wasn't happy about it, but I knew I had to accept the fact that we'd have a non-paying tenant until the lizard chose otherwise.

I decided that if we were going to live together, I should give it a name. Calvin had called it a "she" but I don't think he could really have known. I settled on the gender-neutral "Scaley" and decided that it would go about its business, and I would go about mine. There was nothing to fear. Like most things in my new life, it would just take a little getting used to.

In the days and weeks that followed, I was delighted to discover that Scaley wasn't the only creature that had settled in and around our little lodge. Our thatched roof held a lovely surprise — a family of bushbabies! These tiny primates with enormous eyes and long tails spent their days slumbering in the thatch, emerging each evening to catapult through the trees as they went off to find food in the form of insects and tree sap.

Groups of spotted guineafowl with their distinctive blue heads and bright-red wattles would visit at dawn and again at dusk to gobble up the seed I put down for them and other bird visitors. The smaller, more skittish francolins were also regulars, earning their reputation as the bush alarm clock, their calamitous call signalling the dawn of each new day, and then calling it a day as dusk settled in.

The large concrete birdbath we'd brought from our old place was installed atop an old tree trunk we'd made into a table. It was quickly becoming a favourite spot for bulbuls, paradise flycatchers, kingfishers and colourful purple-crested louries, to name just a few.

I couldn't wait for Johann to get home again so he could enjoy our new home and all the creatures that had come with it.

I still missed Johann, but our months apart had taken on a different rhythm for me. Thirty days had once felt like an eternity and I'd struggled to fill the time, but that had changed completely. I was making some good friends; Hoedspruit seemed to be a magnet for interesting and creative souls. My new tribe included Colleen, who created funky but rustic furniture using wood from old pallets; Jackie, who'd bravely bought a farm on her own and was striving to live off the grid; and Maureen, a former actress, dancer and stuntwoman-turned-choreographer who'd created a singing, drumming and dancing group called Roots of Rhythm. With such vibrant company, I was starting to enjoy a social life again.

Also, in addition to my volunteer teaching at Tanda Tula, I had another project to keep me busy, creative and focused.

It had started out as a project that Johann and I could do together, combining my photography, Johann's considerable artistic ability and my love of elephants. I'd wanted to call it "A Guy, A Girl and an Elephant", and the plan was to create original art on a unique canvas: elephant-dung paper to sell as souvenirs to tourists.

Because elephants have such a poor digestive system, the grass they eat comes out the other end mostly intact. After boiling it in caustic soda and adding water, it becomes a paste that can be spread evenly across a screen and dried in the sun to create rustic-looking handmade paper. We'd sell the art as souvenirs to tourists and donate part of the proceeds to Elephants Alive, a local elephant-conservation project.

I'd thought it would be great fun to work together, but Johann was reluctant, to say the least. He'd studied graphic design prior to becoming a medic, and one of his instructors had failed him not once but twice on the painting component of the course. Looking at the work in his old portfolio, I just couldn't understand it. The sketches and paintings were beautiful.

"The teacher just didn't like my style, and refused to pass me," Johann theorized, and explained, "They wouldn't allow me to carry that subject forward into the third year, so that was the end of that."

Since that time, Johann hadn't picked up a pencil, paintbrush or sketch pad. I tried to convince him that one person's opinion was just that, and that he shouldn't let it extinguish his creativity, but I truly could empathize with him, as I had also abandoned art because of the influence of a teacher.

When I was 8 years old, I'd begged my parents to let me take art lessons, and despite a very tight budget, they'd allowed me to give it a try. They signed me up with a nun at the local convent, a very gifted drawer and painter. Unfortunately, her talents didn't extend to teaching. For our first lesson she put a bowl of fruit on the table and asked me to draw it. I was very nervous under her watchful eye, and I quickly erased my first several attempts in embarrassment. By the end of that lesson, she'd already concluded that I didn't have much talent.

The rest of our lessons went like this: she would present me with a subject to draw; I would try for about half an hour; then she would take over, commandeering the box of oil pastels and turning my amateur renderings into passable pieces of art. At the end of our time together I'd amassed quite a portfolio of artworks — none of them mine.

The "you have no talent" message had been fully received, and I put the sketch pad and pastels in a box in the basement, where they remained until they were thrown out when I left for college.

My passion for art had been rekindled in South Africa. You can't help but be inspired by the glorious sunsets, the scenery, the majestic animals and the beautiful faces, bright smiles and colourful clothing of the people. I'd dabbled in lessons for a little while but found myself floundering and rapidly losing confidence. Luckily, I met someone who helped me to see things differently.

Nicola crashed my birthday party — that's the story she tells, anyway. Since we were the only two Canadians living in Hoedspruit, mutual friends thought we should meet, and she'd actually been invited to a small surprise cake-and-coffee gathering for me. But because she didn't actually know me, she felt quite awkward showing up.

We had a lot in common, not least our inability to work legally in South Africa. We were both making the most of this forced work hiatus, using it to explore our creativity.

As our friendship grew, Nicola encouraged me by word and example to find my own artistic niche. She created her paintings of Africa's scenery and wildlife, large and small, on a base of newspaper collage, brought to life with paint and other materials like sandpaper and foil. Her work was charming, quirky and absolutely engaging. Her paintings always made me smile.

"I'm not a great painter," she'd say, modestly, "but I do something so different that nobody can tell me I'm doing it wrong. That's what you need to do — create your own thing."

That's how I got excited again about the concept of combining my photographs with art on elephant-dung paper — it certainly would be different!

Johann graciously agreed to give it a try and we worked at it for a while, but it became obvious that his heart wasn't in it, so we abandoned the project. If it wasn't going to be fun — and clearly it wasn't — there was no point in doing it.

Soon after we'd given up the project, I went to a local art show, and was introduced there to a striking young woman with long raven hair, friendly blue eyes and a shy smile. Alicia was also new to the area. She'd left behind a career in horticulture, and her husband Rob had sold the family farm on the outskirts of Pretoria to move their family to our small, close-knit community. Hoedspruit seemed to be an incubator for creativity, and her talent was clearly blossoming. Alicia had only started to paint a few years before when, after the death of her father, she'd felt absolutely compelled to buy paint, brushes and canvas. The pain of his passing had awakened a new passion, and revealed a natural talent unlike anything I'd ever seen.

As we got to know each other over the next few months, it occurred to me that we'd make a great team. Alicia was so good at painting everything that she had a hard time deciding what to paint. I had the vision to create images, but lacked the ability to bring them to life on canvas. I was sure that together we could create something amazing — and so "Two Girls and an Elephant" was born.

Johann's long absences were no longer something to dread, but had become an opportunity for creative play and experimentation. Alicia and I learned from each other, and through trial and error eventually came up with our first collection of oil-on-canvas paintings which we planned to print on elephant-dung paper. The modern, brightly coloured pieces inspired the slogan "African art with attitude", which we planned to use in our advertising once we finally had a product to sell.

I was having fun and learning about art but, more importantly, I was proving a theory that I'd been starting to believe about life: there was no longer any doubt in my mind that I was creating my own reality.

This concept was a huge revelation for me. I'd lived the first part of my life as I suspect most people do: showing up each day and reacting to the things that happened. Yes, I had goals and plans, but it seemed to me that those were at the mercy of outside events and other people. I didn't understand that my thoughts and my beliefs actually influenced the events that occurred in my life, as well as the people who came into it.

I'd been introduced to this line of thinking initially in the "Conversations with God" books by Neale Donald Walsch, and the same idea kept cropping up in all of the spiritual reading I'd been doing in the last few years. It was an intriguing theory, both exciting and disturbing: exciting, if it were true that by changing my thoughts I could change my life; and disturbing, because if I was, in fact, creating my experience, I had only myself to blame for all the drama and trauma that had occurred in my life.

I didn't like that idea at all. It meant that I must in some way have been responsible for the complete collapse of my career and my previous marriage. That was hard to swallow — it felt much better to put the blame on other people and circumstances. And on the surface it just didn't make any sense. Why would I repeatedly press the self-destruct button on my life?

I thought about my career. Back when I first fell in love with radio, I was barely a teenager, and it was a very different business then, creative and fun. But that had changed. Now, radio was very formulaic. We called it "McRadio" — just as McDonald's has a set way to make a hamburger, there's a set way for radio-show hosts to pass an hour: play current song, one minute for weather, two minutes for traffic, time check, insert something interesting or funny for three minutes, go to commercials.

I'd gone into broadcasting to entertain, educate and inspire, but that no longer seemed to be the mandate. The content of programmes was now largely dictated by high-priced broadcasting consultants.

The head honchos of our radio network had hired one from the United States. How we dreaded her visits! The last time she'd come to town to critique Dave's and my on-air performance, she'd insisted that we needed to spend our time talking about the latest reality-TV show. I really didn't see the point. If you liked *Dancing with the Stars*, you watched it. If you didn't like it, why would you want to listen to people talking about it on the radio? So much of what the consultant — and, ultimately, the station management — wanted us to do seemed silly and superficial to me.

By that stage, I'd been an on-air personality for twenty-five years. I still enjoyed the people I worked with, and I was finally at the point where it paid well, so I never would've quit, but I had to admit that in the years leading up to my dismissal, I hadn't been finding my career truly fulfilling for quite some time.

Then I thought about my marriage, and about some other relationships that had faded away. Maybe we just didn't fit any more. And if that were the case, there was no need for me to feel hurt, abandoned or a failure. It was just time for that part of my life to end, and because I hadn't been prepared to make the tough decisions, life had graciously supplied me with all those endings. They were painful endings, to be sure, but that's often how new beginnings are born.

As the old saying goes, pain is inevitable but suffering is optional. I had to acknowledge that I'd chosen to suffer for far too long over what I'd perceived to be losses.

Once I'd fully digested these insights, I made a conscious effort to trust the flow of life. I accepted that if something or someone left my life, it was simply part of a natural evolution. The universe abhors a vacuum, so the space that was created by the departure would soon be filled by something or someone else. My job was to give attention to what I *did* want, and to not give much thought or energy to the things I didn't want or the things I didn't have.

I made it my mission to prove to myself that what you focus on expands in your experience, whether it's wanted or unwanted. And as I started to really pay attention to my thoughts and to live purposefully, I continued to see the proof unfolding in my life.

The pattern was perfectly clear in the events of the previous several months. Instead of dwelling on our deteriorating lifestyle at Ver End, I'd focused my attention on finding a new, wonderful place to live. And it had worked — I was living in it. What's more, it had come with a completely unexpected bonus: we now had "traversing rights" on a neighbouring property that was a game farm, meaning that we could go there on game drives any time we wanted.

Instead of focusing on the disappointment of Johann and I not managing to work together to create art, I'd purposefully focused my attention on my desire to create. Lo and behold, the right collaborator had appeared to bring my idea to life.

That was already proof enough for me to carry on with my new line of thought. I was really starting to believe that if I did my part, the universe would look after the details, lining up the right people, events and circumstances to support my desires. It felt good to know that the universe had my back.

Even with this new awareness, it was still all too easy to slip back into old, well-worn thought patterns. I acknowledged that, and tried not to be too hard on myself when I found I was worrying about and fixating on things I didn't want. I'd stop, and decide to choose a better thought. It soon became obvious that if I did that, it was never long before another better thought came along to join the first one, and the momentum would shift. I felt empowered knowing that I was consciously shaping my life.

My trips to Tanda Tula safari camp were the highlight of every week. The adult-literacy programme for the staff was well into its second year, and the progress was remarkable. Some of the staff who hadn't even understood the concept of an alphabet when we started were now reading at about a grade-two level. Many who hadn't known how to hold a pencil were printing neatly on lined paper. The more advanced were tackling the basics of grammar, learning about nouns, verbs, adjectives and adverbs.

Our star pupil was Melina, a woman of undetermined age (there seemed to be no record of her birth). I was told that when she'd tried to get some form of government ID, the official had looked at her and as a best guess assigned to her a year of birth that would make her 55 years old. The reality was that she was much older, but this clerical lapse of judgment meant that Melina wouldn't reach the mandatory retirement age of 65 and be able to draw a government pension for quite some time.

Melina was the queen of the Tanda Tula laundry room, unofficially but firmly in charge of the other women who washed and ironed the bedding, towels, tablecloths and napkins for the lodge, and the laundry for the guests. Everything that left the laundry room was immaculate and perfectly pressed. Much serious conversation seemed to be going on while the women worked, but of course they spoke Shangaan, a dialect of the Tsonga language, so we never knew what they were saying. Camp manager Hayley used to joke that if the South African government were ever overthrown, the plot would likely have been hatched in the Tanda Tula laundry room!

Melina's status as a leader meant that when she'd decided to investigate the adult-literacy programme, all the others had followed suit. Melina had been very wary of the education programme at first: she obviously wanted to learn to read and write, but I think she wasn't quite sure what to make of the white woman from Canada who'd showed up to help teach her. She sat stone-faced throughout the lessons, and answered grudgingly if I asked a question. She tried to hide her interest and enthusiasm, but it was obvious that she was very clever and was learning quickly. I knew that she'd be able to learn even faster and would be a great help to her co-workers if I could just get her to let down her guard.

Over time, it had happened. Now, Melina smiled often, and it always made my day if I could get her to laugh. She was helping the other women with their studies, as was the beautiful Clenny.

Clenny was rarely able to make it to the formal classes, as the timing didn't fit into her workday schedule. She was bright, educated and well spoken, and had found her niche at Tanda Tula. She worked in the office, making sure the personalized welcome letters to the guests were printed, neatly rolled and tied with a raffia ribbon, and placed in their rooms before they arrived. She oversaw the cleaning staff, and would also help out hosting at breakfast for the guests at the outdoor kitchen in the bush where the meal was served after the early-morning game drive.

This was a much better use of her many talents than her previous jobs had been. She'd gone from petrol-station attendant to curio-shop clerk, then finally to Tanda Tula where she was hired as a housekeeper. It hadn't taken long for her potential to shine through, and she was promoted, quickly climbing her way up to her current position.

She was loved and respected by the entire staff. A short, round woman with a smile as wide as her hips, she was the embodiment of beauty — on this side of the world, anyway. She was absolutely proud and confident, with a bold fashion sense apparent from her colourful headscarf down to her matching shoes. In my view, the western standard of beauty paled by comparison.

Despite the scheduling conflict with the formal classes, Clenny was keen to learn and often asked me for advanced assignments to help her improve her English vocabulary. She was delighted to be introduced to Mma Ramotswe, Mma Makutsi and the other characters in Alexander McCall Smith's *No 1 Ladies' Detective Agency* series of books.

Clenny was also becoming more proficient on the computer, and her warm, outgoing personality was fast making her a favourite with the guests. She was being given more responsibility and was invited to be one of the hosts at dinner, a role normally filled by owners Nina and Don, managers Hayley and Dale, and the rangers who were needed to provide an armed escort to take the guests back safely to their tents for the night.

Hosting was something I got to do as well, on the nights that I stayed over to teach two days in a row. When Clenny and I hosted together, it was a great opportunity to watch her in action, and to coach her in the art of conversing with people from all over the world.

I helped Clenny; however, she helped me more. The language barrier remained an issue when I was teaching. Despite my best efforts and intentions, I struggled to make myself understood in English and the smattering of Shangaan words I'd mastered. That's where Clenny came in. If I felt a lesson hadn't been well understood, I could always rely on her to take it up again in the staff quarters in the evening when the laundry-room posse were doing their homework.

Before too long, it was decided that since she was hosting dinners, Clenny should also help out at the bar when the guests arrived back from the late-afternoon game drive. This led to one of my favourite lessons of all time. Clenny wasn't at all familiar with alcohol, imbibing only occasionally a glass of wine or a tot of sweet Amarula, the iconic South African liqueur made from the fruit of the marula tree.

One morning I took her down to the bar and pulled out every bottle of spirits on hand. I poured small tasters of each, and Clenny sampled them by turn, often just dipping in her finger in order to have the smallest amount and still get a sense of the taste. For the most part, the samples drew a grimace, but she did concede that some wouldn't be too bad with the right mix. She dutifully took notes as I explained which mixes were generally used with each of the spirits.

"Vodka is, I think, nature's most perfect alcohol," I joked. "You can mix it with almost anything: tonic or soda or, if you prefer something sweeter, fruit juice, 7-Up or Sprite."

"Yes, I think something a bit sweeter could work for me," Clenny said.

"How about vodka and Amarula?"

"Only if there's someone to carry me home," she deadpanned.

We laughed a lot, but in the end the session proved very productive and we compiled a handy bar guide she could keep stashed under the counter for quick reference.

I found teaching became even more interesting when I could help the women to communicate in ways useful for them in their everyday lives, and in their jobs. With the less advanced, I covered the phrases they were most likely to use when sending a text message (or SMS, as we call them in South Africa). I taught terminology used at the grocery store and the bank.

Most exciting of all, I was able to use my nature-guide training to help some of the guides prepare for their national exams. Of course, their knowledge about the wildlife and the environment totally eclipsed mine, but having written the test a few years earlier, I was in a position to teach them the terminology required to pass a very challenging exam in a language that wasn't their own.

I was creating my life, and I loved the life I was creating. I had challenging, fulfilling work, great friends and a wonderful marriage, but with Johann still away every other month, I knew I still had some work to do.

I wanted to have it all — all at the same time.

Scaley and guineafowl visitors to our garden

Nicola and I

Alicia and I at our first exhibition

Star pupil Melina gets her diploma from Nina

Tanda Tula school's first graduation

Clenny

Chapter 3

Ready, fire, aim!

That's the approach Johann and I had taken when we'd decided to elope, not knowing where we'd live or how we'd make it work. We knew we wanted to build a life together, and the only way to do that was to take a leap of faith and plunge in. If you wait for the conditions to line up and for the path to be completely clear, you could wait a very long time.

We decided to adopt the same attitude towards Johann moving home, so he gave his notice in Mozambique. He'd have to work only one more month-long stint.

We'd managed to save up enough money to cover our living expenses for a few months, and to make what we hoped would be a smart investment. We went into the granadilla (passionfruit) business.

Our partners in this endeavour were Alicia and Rob. With her background as a horticulturalist and Rob's as a farmer, they had they expertise. When they'd moved to Hoedspruit they'd rented some land not far from our old place at Ver End. They were growing baby vegetables — baby marrows, squash and sweetcorn — and occasionally trying their luck with tomatoes. They were getting by, but barely. They wanted to add granadillas to their crop because they had the potential to be quite lucrative. The problem was that they lacked the lump sum of money to get started.

That's where we came in. We'd managed to get ourselves on a better financial footing, and decided to use our savings to buy three thousand plants, and the wires and poles that would support the growing vines. Rob and Alicia would cover the cost of the land rental, irrigation and staff, and before long we hoped the big money would start rolling in.

It was a great plan in theory. But I knew from the experiences of farmer friends in Canada that agriculture is a risky business, and you can't count your chickens (or your granadillas) before they hatch.

After we'd made the decision to go into business with our friends, I remembered the prophecy of the sangoma, the traditional healer I'd consulted a year before. Part doctor, part psychologist and part fortune-teller, she'd thrown the bones onto her sacred mat, read the signs and, with the help of her ancestors and mine, gazed into my future. She'd said that Johann and I would go into business with a man and a woman, and that the business would have something to do with food. At the time I couldn't imagine how that would come to pass, but obviously she'd been right!

I tried to set aside any doubts about the success of the venture and focus on the miraculous fact that Johann was home for the month, and would be going back to Mozambique only one more time before coming home for good. Now it was his turn to get intimately acquainted with the menagerie living in our roof and all around the property. He seemed suitably impressed by my acceptance of Scaley, the enormous monitor lizard. We'd sometimes catch sight of him in the garden when he left his residence in the attic to go and forage for food.

We soon started to explore the property where we had our traversing rights. It was home to a lodge called Khaya Ndlovu, which means "house of the elephant". The prospect of seeing elephants in what we now considered to be our own back garden was pretty exciting!

We spent many happy hours cruising along the rocky roads, crisscrossing the property in search of animals and finding the places with the best views for sundown drinks. Soon we had three favourite spots: a lookout high on the riverbank with an expansive view of the mountains and the riverbed below, the sandy floor of the dry riverbed at a place called Rhino Crossing, and at the water's edge at Hippo Dam where we often saw hippos at play. Their urgent braying and grunting became one of my favourite sounds — it sounded so much like laughter you couldn't help but join in.

As we were making our way home one evening, Johann suddenly hit the brakes.

"Do we know if there are lions on the property?" he asked.

I didn't think there were, but that's the thing about the bush — you never know what you might come across. Fences can be deterrents, but they're no guarantee, especially when it comes to keeping out big cats. We backed up slowly and sure enough, there was a male lion, sitting sphinx-like in the grass. Next to his front paws we saw a tail flick, then a head popped up. A female rolled over and sat up next to the male. Beside her, a pair of back paws shot out from the tall grass as a young male stretched and yawned.

I grabbed my camera and started shooting, hoping there was still enough light for photos. As the sun went down, we watched the pride wake up. Eventually we could pick out five silhouettes in the twilight. We watched them playfully interacting and grooming each other until the group wandered off into the thicket, likely looking for their next meal. And so ended another extraordinary ordinary day in Africa!

We thought we'd met all the regulars in and around our lodge but one day we got quite a surprise. I was standing at the kitchen sink, washing dishes, and Johann was on drying duty. Out the window, colour and movement caught my eye. Johann had seen it too: something vibrant-blue was moving through the dull, dead grass. Then we saw a flash of green, and eyes — dozens of them! It came closer, and we realized it was a large bird — a peacock.

Not what you'd expect in the South African bushveld, but there he was, as bold and beautiful as could be.

He carried on past the window and headed straight to the patch of dirt behind the house where we scattered seed for the usual customers, the guineafowls and francolins. The peacock may have been new here, but he seemed to know his way around.

We moved out to the back patio and watched him peck away at the ground, pausing every now and then to raise his head to check that we were still standing at a safe distance. It didn't take him long to decide that there was nothing to fear, and he hopped up onto the patio. Then, flapping his enormous wings, he jumped up and found a perch on the wooden pole we'd installed as a safety rail.

We were absolutely delighted but mystified. Where had he come from? Was he alone or were there others?

From then on, the peacock became a regular visitor, often stopping by two or three times a day.

As we observed his behaviour, it became clear that he was in fact alone, and he was desperate to change that: we could tell by his numerous displays that he was actively seeking a mate.

Unfortunately, he was looking for love in all the wrong places. He'd fan out his impressive tail feathers to strut his stuff in front of our large aloe plant every time he came by. It was a glorious display, but sadly wasted on the plant, which he seemed to mistake for a prospective mate.

"That guy needs a girl," Johann observed.

"And to have his eyes tested," I said.

Enquiries around the other lodges on the property didn't shed any light on how the peacock had come to roost at Raptors' Lodge. By all accounts he'd just turned up one day and decided to stay.

I did, however, find out his name. Tanja, the lovely woman who oversaw the bookings for the rental of the lodge units, explained to me that the Afrikaans word for peacock is *pou*, pronounced "po", so he'd been dubbed Paulus – Paul in Afrikaans. The name seemed to suit him.

Johann and I were really enjoying our time together at home, and we were preparing for what would happen after he finished his final rotation in Mozambique. He'd been looking for work on several online job sites but it seemed his current qualifications weren't going to land him a decent job. He signed up to take a couple of courses, advanced cardiac life support and international trauma life support, which combined would surely bolster his resume. He was excited, and I was too — the courses were in Cape Town and I was going to go with him.

We'd visited Cape Town for my birthday in the spring, and I was completely captivated by the city and its happy, friendly inhabitants. Its physical beauty is beyond compare, with majestic Table Mountain at its heart and breathtaking ocean views everywhere you look.

I'd grown up on the waters of Georgian Bay in Ontario. The name of my home town, Penetanguishene, is a First Nations word meaning "land of the rolling white sand". There were more than a dozen beautiful white-sand beaches within a half hour's drive of town. As much as I loved the South African bush, I missed the beach.

The Cape's magnificent scenery was home to some equally magnificent wildlife. I was excited when I spied seals sunning themselves on the rocks in the harbour; and when we went to Boulders Beach to swim with the adorable African penguins, it was one of the best days of my life.

In addition to all that, Cape Town also offered museums and art galleries, theatres, and no end of shops, restaurants and nightclubs showcasing a vibrant music scene. The wine regions of Stellenbosch and Franschhoek were just a stone's throw away. I couldn't wait to get back there and do more exploring.

A few days before Johann's course was to begin, we started our journey, driving the five hours from Hoedspruit to Johannesburg to catch a flight to Cape Town. When we landed in the Mother City, we picked up a rental car and, with the help of the GPS, made our way to the suburb of Plumstead, where we'd found affordable accommodation in a small cottage in the back garden of a charming home. Our hosts greeted us and showed us to our quarters, a compact room that was kitchenette, dining room and bedroom. The tiny bathroom was concealed by a sliding door. It was cramped but perfect for our purposes.

We had the next day to ourselves and decided to take full advantage of it to visit Robben Island, site of the prison where former South African president Nelson Mandela had spent eighteen of his twenty-seven years of incarceration. The island is a popular tourist attraction where tours are given by former inmates, some of whom actually served time with the great man.

Mandela often credited his time in that prison as the catalyst for his transformation from the angry young man he'd been when he was arrested in 1962, into the wise statesman who spent the rest of his life advocating for peace and reconciliation. I was keen to learn more about that period of his life.

We boarded the ferry at the V&A Waterfront for the journey across Table Bay to the infamous island. It was a distance of only twelve kilometres, but to the political prisoners who were being held there it must have felt like they'd been banished to the dark side of the moon. In the beginning they'd had no contact with the outside world. Over time, and through great patience under Mandela's leadership, the prisoners had been permitted to write and receive one letter every six months. Once a year, a thirty-minute visit by a family member was allowed.

We were met by a guide who ushered our group on to one of the waiting buses. The tour began with a drive around the island. Eventually the guide took us to the limestone quarry where Mandela and his fellow inmates had done hard labour each day. I tried to imagine how it must have felt, repeatedly swinging a pick-axe in the relentless heat of the midday sun made even more intense by its reflection off the white rock. The glare was literally blinding; Mandela's vision had been permanently impaired as a result of the time he spent breaking rock from that quarry face. And breathing in the limestone dust caused damage to the lungs.

Worst of all though, I suspect, was the damage to the psyche and the soul. Prisoners were banned from singing while they worked, to make sure that the sheer monotony of the task was as punishing as the physical strain.

From the quarry we moved on to the prison itself. Another guide came out to meet us — a man who'd also been a political prisoner when Mandela was being held there. He began the tour in the mess hall, where several menus still hung on the walls. We were surprised to learn that skin colour even played a role in how the men were fed. Their race determined how much and what type of food they received: the quantity and quality of the food doled out to the black prisoners was less than and inferior to that given to the Asian prisoners and to those of mixed race.

Soon we were lined up in the corridor leading to the cell that prisoner number 46664 had called home for so many years. Due to the large number of people on the tour, we would each have only a moment to look into the cell and snap a photo. I expected the space to be small and sparse but still actually seeing it came as a shock. It was less than two square metres in area, and it contained only a bedroll, a small stool and a ceramic pot. I wondered how many times Mandela must have looked longingly out that window and wondered if he would ever be free.

For the first time it occurred to me that he'd been locked away there just after I was born and that he'd looked out that window every day until after I turned 18. Even then he wasn't liberated; he was just transferred to another prison in order to isolate him from the other inmates in the hope that, alone, he'd be easier for the government to manipulate. Of course, that strategy didn't work but it would take another eleven years until his long walk to freedom was finally complete.

Being in that place and hearing the stories of other prisoners was a very emotional experience for me, but it was a big eye-opener for my husband.

Mandela had been sent to prison before Johann was even born. Despite having grown up in a very politically liberal household, for most of the years of Mandela's incarceration,

Johann wasn't even aware of the man's existence. The then government's news-censorship policy was highly effective — the citizens were kept in the dark. It wasn't until the world turned its attention to South Africa and began boycotts aimed at freeing political prisoners that most South Africans started to have an inkling of what was going on. When people did start to find out about Mandela, he was simply branded a terrorist who deserved to be in jail.

When the much more complex truth started to leak out, the treatment of political prisoners didn't seem so harsh. The population was told that prison conditions weren't that bad, that Mandela was receiving an education and that he had a television in his cell. Of course, through his determination and persistence, Mandela had won those rights for prisoners over time.

Johann had never been told about the hard labour and the degree of humiliating and inhumane treatment prisoners had been subjected to in the beginning. Seeing the prison for himself and hearing the truth from others who'd been incarcerated there, some at the same time as Mandela, made my husband feel very disappointed in the white authorities he'd blindly trusted in his youth. He was even quieter than usual as we rode the ferry back to the mainland.

The next morning Johann was up and out early to start his course. Because we were staying some distance from the city centre, I'd planned to stay home for the day and use the time to dabble at writing and practise drawing. I continued to look at my not being able to legally work in South Africa as a gift of time, and I was determined to take advantage of it by taking another run at pursuits I'd long ago abandoned. We'd planned to drive into the city that evening and take a stroll around the bustling V&A Waterfront, and I was very much looking forward to the excursion.

I flipped on the television to find a local weather forecast. Instead, I heard the devastating news: former South African president Nelson Mandela had died.

We'd been hearing rumours about his ill health for months, and one media outlet had actually confirmed his death some six months previously, but then had quickly recanted the report. That error in journalistic judgment had created more rumours, including one that claimed Mandela was in fact clinically dead but was being kept alive by machines while his greedy family members scrambled to secure their claims on his fortune.

There'd also been much speculation about what might happen when the dreaded event actually did occur, when the nation's beloved father, Tata Madiba, finally took his last breath. Some said his death would trigger an apocalyptic "Night of the Long Knives" or "Operation White Clean Up", in which the fury of tens of thousands of angry blacks would be unleashed, and they would go on a murderous spree, targeting every white person in sight. According to a white-supremacy group that seemed to exist solely to promote this conspiracy theory, the killing would start in Johannesburg, then move to Pretoria before spreading like wildfire across the entire country.

The first time I'd heard about this supposed plot I was at Tanda Tula. It had started out as a normal day and I was sitting at the long table on Don and Nina's porch, preparing lessons and awaiting the arrival of the laundry-room ladies for the first class of the day. Linneth was the first to arrive, and she was visibly upset.

"Have you heard the news?" she asked.

"What news?"

"He's gone. Tata Madiba is gone."

I was surprised at the intensity of my reaction. My gut churned and tears sprang to my eyes. Even though Mandela hadn't been politically active since he'd retired in 2004, and had rarely even been seen in public since the World Cup in 2010, the world had seemed to me to be a better place just because he was still in it.

Before the shock of the news had even sunk in, however, another report was issued saying that reports of Mandela's death weren't true. He was still with us.

Of course, the incident inspired a lot of conversation around the camp that day, and it was Smiling, one of the bartenders, who told me about the apparently impending doom for the white population when Mandela did die. "It's going to be awful," he said. "I'm glad we're up here in the bush, because on the day it does happen, I'm going to arm myself and go off and hide."

My friend, ranger Scotch, happened to stroll into the bar at that point in the conversation. "You, in the bush with a gun? You'd probably end up shooting yourself. You wouldn't last a night!" he said teasingly. "What are you talking about anyway?"

"The Night of the Long Knives, man!" Smiling exclaimed.

"Oh, c'mon, don't tell her things like that. You're scaring her," Scotch said. "It's all nonsense, anyway. First they said it would happen when Mandela was released from prison in 1990. Then they said it would happen after the 1994 election. It didn't happen then, and it's not going to happen now."

I agreed with Scotch's assessment. Yes, there were black people who hated white people, and white people who hated black people, but in my experience the vast majority of the South African people wanted to follow Mandela's shining example: to let go of bitterness and to build a peaceful, prosperous life for all.

That day in Plumstead in Cape Town, when I learned that Mandela had indeed died, the prediction was proven false once and for all. No sinister plot was set in motion. There was only sadness at the passing of South Africa's beloved son, and gratitude for the legacy of reconciliation he'd left behind.

I watched the news all day, as the tributes poured in from around the world. The story of Nelson Mandela's amazing life was recounted and analyzed a dozen different ways by the presenters on the national television channels.

When Johann came back from his day of classes, we decided to head into the city to the Grand Parade, the main public square where Mandela had first addressed South Africans after his release from prison. In that speech he'd said that it was because of the tireless and heroic sacrifices of the people that he'd been freed, and that for that reason he was putting the remaining years of his life in their hands. True to his word, in 1994 he became the country's first truly democratically elected leader, committed to the idea of a rainbow nation where there was equality and opportunity for all.

Now, on the day of his death, mourners were being invited to gather at that historic place, members of the rainbow nation coming together for an interfaith evening of prayer. This was a big moment in history, and we were so glad to be there to be part of it.

Thousands of people had flocked to the square that Thursday evening. They were black, white, coloured, Indian and Asian, young and old, rich and poor, all coming together to pay tribute to the man who was regarded as the father of us all. I'd expected the mood to be sombre, but the mourning would come later. That night was all about celebrating a remarkable life. There was chanting, dancing and singing.

There are so many images etched in my mind from that remarkable gathering. Women perched on the shoulders of their partners, waving the South African flag. A group of young girls wearing matching T-shirts proudly displayed the colourful signs they'd made, with "Tata Madiba" boldly painted in bright yellow; they sang beautifully and waved their signs enthusiastically. A young couple, a white man and a black woman, with their arms wrapped around each other, cloaked themselves in a swathe of shweshwe-style fabric imprinted with Mandela's beaming face.

The coming Sunday was declared a national day of prayer. Johann had to write his exams, so I asked him to drop me off in the city centre at St George's Cathedral, the church of Archbishop Emeritus Desmond Tutu. I arrived before the first mass, and found a seat near the front. Tutu had said a mass there for his dear friend just two days earlier, and I hoped the religious leader I'd long aspired to see in person would still be there.

The seats started to fill up quickly, and a woman with her two young children sat down beside me. I saw several television reporters take their positions close to the pulpit.

"Maybe he's here!" I thought to myself but I must have said it out loud because the young woman beside me leaned in and whispered, "No, I'm afraid he's not. He left yesterday for Pretoria."

A little embarrassed, I whispered back, "Oh, of course. I was just really hoping to see him. I have so much admiration and respect for him. It would've been wonderful to see him in person and hear him speak."

"He's a great man," she said, nodding in agreement.

When the priest who was to say the mass approached the pulpit, the TV reporters were obviously disappointed. They recorded the first few minutes of the service and quickly went on their way.

As I listened, I was far from disappointed. The priest spoke eloquently about Mandela, then gave us a candid glimpse into the personal life of the man, reading from letters sent from Mandela to his wife Winnie while he was in prison.

I'd previously regarded the former Mrs Mandela as evil incarnate, but after listening to the content of the letters I gained some insight into what had happened to her during his time in prison, and with this new information it now felt impossible to judge her so harshly. She'd been beaten and humiliated at the hands of the police. They'd taken away her husband, and she too was put in jail on several occasions. The circumstances for both husband and wife were really too much for anyone to bear, and each found a way to cope. Nelson chose love and forgiveness, while Winnie opted to fuel herself with hatred and revenge. It occurred to me that under the same circumstances, many of us would have gone Winnie's route.

In one of the letters Mandela said that the only thing the apartheid government had ever taken away from him was Winnie. She'd been completely changed by all she'd had to endure.

As the mass was ending, the young woman beside me began to cry. People started to file out of the church, and I wasn't sure if I should give her privacy and leave, or stay and try to console her. She sensed my hesitation and touched me on the arm.

"Know why I'm crying, Mma?" she asked. "I'm crying because there's still so much work to do to make Tata Madiba's dream come true. I'm working in the townships just outside of the city, trying to make life better, but there are still so many there with hatred in their hearts."

"Just like Winnie, I guess. Sometimes that seems the best way to cope with the pain. But, of course, it never works."

We sat and chatted a while longer. Her name was Siswe, and she was a social worker.

"Watch for me on TV," she said. "I'm a community activist, and I'm going to be making some noise soon!"

I had no doubt that she would.

She had to be on her way, but she put my number into her phone. We planned to meet up at Cape Town Stadium for the memorial service later in the week.

Soon the crowd filed in for the next mass. Some appeared solemn while others cried openly. I tried to take it all in and learn as much as I could without intruding on people's grief.

Tucked into the pocket of the pew in front of me I saw a programme for the day's masses. Picking it up, I read about the topic of a discussion group that would be held in the foyer following the last service. In keeping with paying tribute to Mandela and the struggles of those who'd worked to end apartheid, the discussion would be about an event had that occurred in 1982, when more than fifty people took shelter in the cathedral to pray and fast to protest their eviction from Nyanga squatter camp on the outskirts of Cape Town.

As I read, I could sense someone's eyes on me. I turned around to see the gentle smile of an elderly black woman. She pointed to a photograph on the page.

"That's me," she said, eyes shining with pride. "I'm Mama Kate. I was there."

"I want to hear all about it," I exclaimed in a whisper, mindful of where we were.

After the third and final mass of the morning, a group of people gathered in the foyer for the chance to hear a first-hand account of determination and bravery as Mama Kate recounted her experience as one of the fifty-seven people who'd taken part in what the media had then labelled a hunger strike.

"They took away our homes and sent us to a 'homeland' where we'd never lived before and where we couldn't find work," Mama Kate said, referring to the apartheid government of the time. "The pittance of money the government gave for the relocation was about enough to get back to Cape Town. They tried to stop us coming back, but we came anyway. And we took refuge within these walls, and said we would go back to our homes or die trying."

The fast had begun on 10 March, and many personal dramas had unfolded during the more than three weeks of its duration. One woman gave birth; another miscarried. Some fasters were taken to hospital suffering from malnutrition. One woman was told by doctors that she was starving to death; undeterred, she came back and resumed the fast.

In an effort to end the sit-in and all the unwanted international media attention it was attracting, the government offered each of the fifty-seven squatters a brick bungalow. They staunchly refused, saying they were fasting not just for themselves but also for all the others who'd been forcibly removed from Cape Town, and who wanted only the right to live and work in peace in the city.

The fast finally ended on 1 April, when a meeting with a government official was arranged. The fasters left the cathedral after they were promised that a decision regarding their demands would be made within three weeks, and that they would be left in peace while they awaited the outcome.

The irony of the agreement being made on April Fool's Day became apparent as the process dragged on for three years.

In the end, the protestors weren't given permission to go back to Nyanga. Many accepted the government's offer to be resettled in a new township being created twenty-five kilometres southeast of Cape Town. They called it Khayelitsha, a name of Xhosa origin meaning "new home". It became the second-largest township in South Africa, after Soweto outside of Johannesburg.

Some of the Nyanga fasters received their houses from the government. Some are still waiting to this day.

The 1982 fast wasn't a complete success, but Mama Kate did credit it as being another step on the path to freedom.

"Did we get everything we wanted? No. But we did get to live with our families and not be hassled by the police. Because of what we did, many others enjoyed this freedom too. I'm proud of what we did," Mama Kate told us. "And today, as we say goodbye to Tata Madiba, I'm even more proud to have been part of the struggle."

Paulus the peacock

With the penguins in Cape Town

The entrance to Robben Island and Nelson Mandela's prison cell

Gathering at the Grand Parade in Cape Town, the day after Nelson Mandela died

Siswe and her children at St George's Cathedral in Cape Town

Mama Kate

Chapter 4

I walked out of the church lost in thought.

I wondered how I would've reacted if I'd been so unfairly treated: banished from my home and denied the opportunity to make a living simply because of the colour of my skin. Would I have protested peacefully as the Nyanga fifty-seven had, or would I have joined a riot, throwing rocks and burning tires in the street?

Both tactics were still being used in South Africa to protest the lack of service delivery. The twentieth anniversary of the democratic election was nearly upon us, but under the African National Congress (ANC) government, conditions for many weren't any better than they'd been under the apartheid regime. In fact, in some cases they were far worse. The standard of education had dropped considerably, and the assurance of free higher education for all remained a distant future goal. The promises of electricity and running water for everyone still hadn't been fulfilled either.

I wondered how Mr Mandela had felt about the performance of the ANC in the twilight years of his life. He'd sacrificed so much to bring the party to power, and he must've been bitterly disappointed at the rampant corruption and the lack of progress two decades on.

I still had several hours to kill while Johann wrote his exams. I wandered around the streets surrounding the cathedral, and eventually came upon a street market. I moved from booth to booth, chatting to the vendors and admiring the handcrafted carvings and beadwork. I found a bright blue T-shirt with an image of Africa on it with a heart placed where Cape Town would be. I paid for it and tucked my souvenir into my knapsack.

I felt around the bottom of the bag to find my phone to check the time. Johann would be about halfway through his first exam. I put the phone and my reading glasses in the outer pocket in the front of the knapsack so they'd be handy when it was time for me to call him later.

I left the market and started making my way back towards the Grand Parade. People were still flocking there to pay their respects and share their grief. The crowd was getting a bit thick, and after being jostled and bumped more than a few times, I decided to take a break from it all and ducked into a fast-food restaurant adjacent to the square. I thought that since it was lunch time, Johann might be on a break, so I decided to give him a call and arrange where and when we would meet later.

I fished around in the front pocket of my knapsack to find my phone and my glasses. The pocket was empty.

I frantically opened the main compartment of the bag. Maybe I'd moved them back and had forgotten? I was sure I hadn't, but I did a thorough search just in case. They'd disappeared!

I was stunned to realize that I'd been robbed.

No sooner had the question "How can that be?" formed in my mind, than the answer became evident: even in my distracted state, I'd noticed a young man following me earlier. When I'd turned to look at him, he'd quickly ducked into one of the stores. I'd seen him again a bit later, but I'd been so absorbed in my own thoughts that I really hadn't paid him much attention. At a street corner I'd had to stop because the traffic light was red, and as I'd stood waiting for it to turn green, another young man had bumped into me. As he apologized, I'd felt another bump from behind. It must have been then that my phone and glasses had been scooped from the pocket of my bag.

I felt overwhelmingly stupid. Cape Town isn't only famous for Table Mountain and penguins. The city is also known to be home to some of the country's most accomplished pickpockets.

The good news was that my wallet was still there. The bad news was that I had no way to contact Johann and, worse still, I couldn't remember the address of the cottage we were renting. I sat there for a while, feeling like a complete idiot. I had no idea what to do.

Then I remembered the advice that all Canadian parents give their children: if you ever get lost or run into trouble, find a policeman. Luckily, I knew just where to find one: there would be about a hundred of them patrolling the Grand Parade.

I left the restaurant and scampered across the street, dodging the cars and the crowd. On the opposite side of the square I spied about a dozen police cars and twice as many men and women in uniform.

I made my way over to them and picked out the friendliest faces. Three officers, two men and a woman, stood chatting and laughing. I was sure I was about to give them something else to laugh about.

We exchanged greetings and I tried to explain my predicament.

"So, you want to use my phone to call your husband?" the woman offered.

"I wish it were that simple," I replied. "You know how when you want to make a call, you just look for the person's name in your phone? That's what I do with everyone, and I now realize that I don't know anybody's phone number, including my husband's!"

"Where are you staying?" asked one of the men.

"Yes, well, you'd think I'd know that too, but I don't. It's in Plumstead, but I don't know the address. I guess when I'm not driving, I really don't pay attention. My husband drove, and I don't have a clue."

I waited for their response, fully expecting that they would collapse to the ground laughing at the absolute idiocy of this ridiculous foreign woman.

"Eish," said the man. "She's a problem!"

"She sure is," I concurred.

"Don't worry, madam, we will sort something out," he said.

"Well, I do have an idea," I ventured. "I do know my husband's email address. Can any of you send email from your phone? Then I could send him a message."

They all agreed that that was a good plan, but none of them had a smartphone, so the two men went off in search of an officer who had one. The woman waited with me.

"I can't even tell you how stupid I feel," I confided.

"It's fine," she said with a reassuring smile.

The two officers soon returned with a third, who was smiling and waving a Blackberry.

"Hello, miss!" he exclaimed. "Here's my phone. You may use it to send a message to your husband."

That led me to my next obstacle. Without my glasses, I couldn't see the keyboard. I had to get the phone's owner to sign into my email and send Johann the message. It took at least half an hour for my address and password to be entered correctly and the message launched into cyberspace. Then there was nothing to do but wait.

An hour passed, and there was no response from Johann. The officers were really concerned. Their shift would be ending in a few hours, and they were determined to see me delivered somewhere safely before they had to leave.

"I know you don't know the address where you're staying, but if we take you to Plumstead and drive around, I'm sure something will look familiar and you will be able to find it," one of the officers suggested.

The other three officers agreed that this was an excellent plan. The five of us piled into one of the patrol cars and set off. By now the shock of the situation had worn off, and I was starting to see the humour in it. Safely nestled between two officers in the back seat of the cruiser, I answered all their questions about Canada and what my life in Africa was like among the animals in the Kruger Park area. None of them had ever been to the park or seen wild animals up close, except in a zoo.

Slowly we wound our way along the suburban streets as I searched for a landmark. Eventually, we passed a sports field that I recognized.

"Oh, turn right here!" I exclaimed.

As we made the turn, the whole street looked familiar and I knew exactly where to go. The officers dropped me off in front of the house and I wondered what the neighbours must have thought of my police escort. I thanked the officers profusely, and they waved a cheery goodbye, satisfied by a job well done. I walked up the driveway, shaking my head at both my incredible stupidity and my ridiculously good luck.

Meanwhile, there was no such relief for Johann. He'd finished his exams and couldn't understand why I hadn't called him, and why I wasn't answering his calls. He tried at least a dozen times, and became more and more frantic at the thought of my having disappeared somewhere in downtown Cape Town. He drove down to the cathedral and checked inside and out, then did a sweep of all the streets in the area. Then he went to the Grand Parade, where he searched in vain.

He'd repeated this whole process three times before the email message from the police officer finally came through. It had apparently been delayed in delivery, which meant that he must have arrived downtown and started his search for me right after the officers and I had left to cruise the streets of Plumstead.

We were reunited at last when he arrived back at the cottage.

He gave me a big hug and a stern talking-to. "Really, love, you're still so Canadian! You've lived here long enough to know that you have to be more aware and more careful!"

"You're right," I agreed, "and I will be in future. I'm just glad that all I lost was my phone and my glasses. I can only imagine how disappointed the thief was when he opened the Ray-Ban case and instead of expensive sunglasses he found my scratched old prescription glasses."

Later that evening it occurred to me that there was something else that had been taken away from me that day: a wonderful opportunity for a potential friendship. I had no way to find Siswe, the woman I'd met at the church, who'd taken my number and was going to call me so that we could meet at Cape Town Stadium for the memorial service. I didn't even know her last name or where she lived. It was a few days before I got a new phone, and I didn't know that I could have kept the same number, and instead I got a new one.

I've often wondered what happened with Siswe's work in the townships, and for a long time I turned on the evening news hoping to catch a glimpse of her, maybe at a rally or a protest. I had no doubt she was out there somewhere, making noise and righting wrongs. There's still a long way to go to create the South Africa Nelson Mandela had believed in so strongly.

Now that Johann's course was finished, our time in Cape Town was rapidly coming to an end. There was still one thing I wanted to do before we left the city. The film version of Nelson Mandela's autobiography, *Long Walk to Freedom*, had just opened in theatres prior to his death. It felt very important that I see it now that the final chapter of his life had been written.

Many people had had the same idea, and we settled in at the crowded cinema to watch this amazing story unfold. In just over two hours and thirty minutes, we saw the cocky, brash, womanizing young lawyer became a political activist, then a political prisoner and ultimately an iconic statesman. It was fascinating and enlightening to witness this transformation so brilliantly portrayed on the big screen.

When the lights went up at the end of the film, I looked to my husband to gauge his reaction. I could tell he was shaken. I tried to draw him into conversation, but he wasn't ready to speak.

We got into the car and drove the half hour back to the cottage mostly in silence.

Eventually, he was ready to talk. "It's one thing to hear about it, but when you see it played out like that, it really makes you understand how bad it was for so many people. And they didn't want violence; they only turned to violence when it seemed they had no choice and that there was no other way to change things.

"I feel disappointed and ashamed of the white authorities for being so blind and clinging to the belief that their white skin made them superior to all other Africans. It's a stubborn traditional Afrikaans belief. I've been told that somewhere in the bible it says that whites are the superior race. Personally I've never been able to find that passage. I feel embarrassed to be associated with the apartheid regime. That's not who I am, or what I believe.

"I'm angry and I'm sad: angry about that belief and sad at all the suffering it caused.

"And I'm angry about the lies. We were told that the people who were part of the struggle were bad people. They weren't bad, they were desperate.

"It's becoming increasingly difficult to excuse my own ignorance. I grew up in a generation that wasn't encouraged to ask questions. When I did find out about Mandela, I asked questions but didn't get good answers. I should've pressed harder to find out more, and I'm angry with myself now because I didn't. I guess it was easier to just believe that he was a terrible person, and that he was getting what he deserved.

"But when the international community imposed sanctions against us, I didn't understand why — I mean, if this guy was such an evil terrorist, why was the world putting pressure on South Africa to set him free? I should've known that there was much more to the story."

"It's a hard pill to swallow, I know," I said. "I got a taste of how you're feeling right now when I learned about the terrible treatment Canada gave its own native people.

"I was always proud to be Canadian. I thought we were this shining example for the world of how people of all races can live in harmony. Then I found out that in the early 1900s, First Nations children were taken away from their parents and put into residential schools for 'aggressive assimilation'. Their cultural practices and beliefs were literally beaten out of them. They were to speak only English or French, and to become Christians. And it's not ancient history — this was still happening in my lifetime, and I was completely ignorant of it while I was going to school.

"The sad fact is that governments only teach you what they want you to know. I only know about it now because when the truth started to come out, Canada formed its own Truth and Reconciliation Commission, just like South Africa did after the abolition of apartheid in 1994."

I felt truly grateful that we were in Cape Town at the time of Madiba's death. The opportunity to talk with people from all walks of life had deepened my understanding of the apartheid struggle in a way that could never have happened by just reading about it. I knew I would never forget being part of the vigil at the Grand Parade, or the morning I'd spent in St George's Cathedral.

The people I met and the stories they told me touched me profoundly. It would've been easy to become overwhelmed with sorrow about the past and fear for the future. But what these brave souls had proven is that where there's pain and fear, there's also resilience and hope.

I decided to focus on that.

One of the helpful police officers on Cape Town's Grand Parade, with Devil's Peak (left) and Table Mountain (right) in the background

Chapter 5

One last time.

Johann packed his bag and left for Mozambique for his final rotation. In thirty days he'd be coming home, and we hoped it wouldn't be long before a better work opportunity came along.

While he was away, I had guests coming. We were settled into our new place, and with our convenient location in town and our beautiful new guest room, it had occurred to us that this could be a new source of income: we could welcome guests to our special corner of the world and show them around.

Before launching into anything, we needed to see if and how it could work. The perfect opportunity arose when a couple from my adopted home city of London, Ontario bought a week's stay at a South African resort in the coastal province of KwaZulu-Natal at a charity auction they'd attended in London. Someone suggested to them that they should contact me to help them round out their trip by travelling north to Limpopo to spend some time with us. It would be great for them to have a local show them all the area's attractions and take them into the Kruger National Park.

Susan and I began chatting via email, and soon we came up with a plan. Before heading to the resort in KwaZulu-Natal, she, her husband Ian and their young son Spencer would travel to Hoedspruit and make their home base with me. I'd provide meals and show them around. The visit would culminate with my taking them to Tanda Tula for four days, where they were sure to have the best possible wildlife experiences.

It would've been perfect if things had gone as planned but you can't control the weather.

It was the end of February, which is late summer in our world. The rainy season should start in November, with most of the rains falling in December, January and early February. However, like elsewhere in the world, the weather just didn't seem to follow the old patterns any more. It had been a dry summer season, but as the time of my guests' arrival drew near, the forecast started predicting heavy rain. If it was accurate, they'd have a couple of nice days when they first arrived, but then the long-overdue rainy season would kick in with a vengeance.

I was in a complete panic. The trip I'd so carefully put together just wasn't going to work. Life in South Africa is lived outdoors, and the activities I'd planned would either have to be cancelled because of the rain, or would just be miserable experiences if we went ahead despite it.

As I studied the carefully constructed itinerary, it occurred to me that there was one thing I might be able to salvage. I called Tanda Tula in the hopes of moving up the family's reservation by a few days. If I picked them up at the airport and took them to the lodge straight away, maybe they would at least be able to get in a few game drives before the rain came down.

I was happy to hear Dolphin's voice on the line when she answered the call. I knew that if there was any way to make this happen, she would be the person to find it.

As she checked the bookings to see if she could accommodate my request, I sat anxiously listening to the sound of her fingers flying over the familiar keys to find the information she needed. Then I heard her chuckle.

"Jax, I don't know how, but you're in luck," she said. "I've had a cancellation for two days just before they're supposed to arrive. I can make it work."

Two days later I met Susan, Ian and Spencer at the airport and explained the change in plans. We drove out to the lodge, and I got them checked in and ready to go on their first game drive. I was thrilled to be able to stay with them to share their first wildlife experience.

With Scotch as our guide, we set out to see what Mother Nature would reveal to us. That day she was nothing short of a show-off!

We soon came on a young male lion at the dam, the first shaggy hints of what would become his mane just starting to show. He was taking a long drink. We watched him lap at the water, then followed him a short distance and discovered why he was so thirsty: he rejoined a companion hunkered down over the carcass of a young buffalo.

Next, we made our way to the den of the spotted hyenas where a couple of exuberant cubs were bouncing all over their caregivers. We suspected the mother was off hunting, as it seemed a couple of subadults had been left to babysit the young ones. Judging by their coloration, the cubs were very young — they still looked like little black puppies, but we could see the beginnings of the spots that would eventually cover their bodies. Playtime soon came to an end when the mother and the other adults returned to the den, then it was the dreaded bath time, with both babies reluctantly submitting to a rigorous tongue-scrub before scampering back into their den for the night.

As is the safari custom, we stopped for drinks and were treated to a spectacular sunset at the dam. Then, to cap things off, more lions — first another young male, and then a mature male with a big mane nuzzling with a female in a dry riverbed.

"That's five lions on your first drive!" exclaimed Scotch. "You're very lucky. But normally when Jacquie's with me on the drive, she's my leopard good-luck charm." Then, turning to me, he chided, "So, where are your leopards, Leopard Lady?"

"Maybe we should change my nickname to Cat Woman, then I can take credit for the lions too," I shot back.

We made our way back to the lodge and settled in for dinner. Scotch and I were hosting, and because there were no fences and animals could roam freely through the camp, it was his duty to provide an armed escort to take the guests safely back to their tents after the meal. The appetizers had been served and he was happily answering questions from young Spencer when he suddenly excused himself from the table. He was gone quite a while, and I wondered what had happened.

Eventually he returned to the table as dessert was being served but he declined his portion. Spencer asked why he hadn't eaten dinner. "Oh, they needed my help in the kitchen, so I ate in there," he explained. I was pretty sure that wasn't what had happened, but I nodded in agreement and the conversation moved on.

Dinner came to an end, and once the last guests had been returned to their tents, I asked Scotch what had happened.

"All of a sudden I felt so sick, I just had to leave," he said. "There's a bug going around camp, and I guess it's my turn. The good news is it doesn't last long — usually about twelve hours, so I should be okay for tomorrow morning's drive."

When we met in the parking lot at dawn the next morning, Scotch seemed fine. It had been a long night, he said, but things had settled down and he was ready to go. As we were about to leave, there was excited chatter on the radio informing us that African wild dogs had been spotted in the area. These beautiful dogs with their colourful, seemingly paint-spattered coats are rare; they're one of the world's most endangered carnivores. On the entire continent there are only about five or six thousand of them, and in South Africa there are only about five hundred.

We headed north to find them, and we were lucky to arrive just in time to see the pack of eight getting worked up for the hunt. There was yipping and chirping, nudging and jumping as they spurred each other on into a frenzy of anticipation. Suddenly, they were off like a shot, and though we followed close behind them, we didn't witness the actual kill. That happens in an instant, when they all set on the prey at once, tearing at it from all sides. This method of hunting may seem far crueller than the tactics used by the big cats, who suffocate their prey, but I've been told that the dogs' method is actually quick and painless, as the prey goes into immediate shock and doesn't feel a thing. Witnessing the feeding frenzy, I hoped that was true.

After that spectacular start, a call over the radio told us that there was a young male leopard lying in a riverbed. We were on our way to see him, when we had to stop — for another leopard! This was a female who'd just killed a small antelope and was moving it to a shady spot to enjoy her breakfast. We watched her for a while, then moved on to see the young male lounging in the riverbed.

I was enjoying the sighting when the cramps hit and I suddenly felt sick. I tapped Scotch on the arm. "What happened to you last night is happening to me now," I whispered urgently.

Nodding his head in sympathy, he turned to the guests and announced, "Let's leave this boy now and go and have some coffee and tea." He set off in the direction of the bush-breakfast spot — not a place he'd normally do a coffee break but there was an outhouse there and he was kindly trying to get me to a toilet as quickly as possible. I prayed we'd make it, not wanting to consider the embarrassment of the alternative.

Our progress was soon interrupted by more news on the radio. There'd been another leopard sighting very close by.

"But we've just had two brilliant sightings — can't we give this one a miss?" I pleaded in desperation.

"No; this one is a leopard in a tree."

Regardless of my dire circumstances, I knew we had to go. A leopard in a tree is probably the most iconic African sighting there is. There was no way we could deny our guests that. My heart sank, and my stomach churned furiously.

By that point I don't know whether I was ghostly white or seasick green. I tried to stay calm, breathe deeply and hope for the best.

The leopard was a magnificent sight, and I tried to focus on that and not on the agitated gurgling of my intestines.

After what seemed like an eternity, we left the leopard sleeping in the high branches. As soon as we were a safe distance away, we pulled over, and Scotch and Patrick the tracker started to set up for the coffee break. I quickly made my way behind a clump of trees at a discreet distance and threw up. And then again. And a third time.

Feeling much relieved, I walked back towards the vehicle, and saw the guests watching my return with looks of shock on their faces. I felt embarrassed, thinking they'd heard my retching, but then realized they were looking behind me, not at me. I turned to see that I was being followed out of the bush by a large hyena. When she saw the group she hesitated, then quickly retreated, loping back into the thicket.

Eventually we made it back to the lodge, and I excused myself to go lie down.

Once fortified with anti-nausea and anti-diarrhoea tablets, I said goodbye to my guests. The forecast still predicted heavy rain, but it looked as if they might get in another game drive or maybe even two before the weather turned.

As I made my way home to Raptors' Lodge, I mentally reviewed all the plans I'd made for the rest of their visit and I wondered if any of them would still be viable in the rain. I'd booked them a trail ride on horseback through one of the wildlife estates; that would be cancelled if the trails were wet, muddy and slippery. The planned visits to the reptile park and the wildlife-rehabilitation centre were both outdoor activities that could go ahead, but really wouldn't be much fun in teeming rain.

I got home and fell into bed, feeling depleted from the stomach virus and anxious about the rest of the family's holiday. Maybe this potential business wasn't such a good idea after all.

I wished Johann were home so that we could talk and he could help me figure out what to do. It was difficult for us to communicate at all, with limited internet and phone signal from his remote camp in northern Mozambique. I had to sort this one out on my own.

Three days later, I was on my way back to Tanda Tula to teach morning classes and to pick up my guests. I marvelled at the miracle — it seemed the rain had held off for their entire four days at the lodge... or had it?

As I approached the river crossing, I was surprised to see water. It hadn't rained in town, but it must have rained farther upstream, and now water was flowing in the normally dry riverbed. I hit the brakes and tried to assess the situation. I knew there was another way into the camp farther north, but I really didn't know how to get there. And I was going to be late if I took a detour.

The water wasn't deep yet and I was in Rover, as we'd affectionately named our Land Rover — wasn't the vehicle made for this sort of thing? And if I crossed at this point now, I could get someone to guide me out on the other route later, if the water continued to rise while I taught my classes and picked up my guests.

It seemed like a perfectly reasonable plan. I decided to go for it. I took my foot off the brake and began to roll down the embankment. Just before I hit the water, I hit the accelerator to increase my momentum and get across.

I almost made it. Just a few metres short of the opposite bank, the left front wheel sank into the thick mud. I was stuck.

I hit the accelerator again, and the tire sank deeper. I tried to reverse but Rover wouldn't budge.

I sat there for a few minutes, trying to think of something — anything — I could do. I grabbed my bag and searched in it for my cellphone. I knew the chance of there being any signal in the area was slim. There was absolutely none.

I pondered my next move. The river was rising, and the water was coming in through the cracks in the doors. It was already covering my ankles.

I wondered what I should do about the engine. Should I leave it running or switch it off? If I switched it off, I may not be able to get it started again. But then, I reasoned, that wouldn't matter because there was no way I was going to be able to drive out anyway. Maybe there would be less damage to the engine if I switched off? I really didn't know the right answer, and I debated for about a minute before deciding that turning it off probably was best. With trepidation, I switched it off.

With the engine silent, all I could hear was the sound of the rushing river. The water inside the vehicle was already up to my knees, and rising fast. It would soon cover the seat. I grabbed my bag and my camera off the passenger seat and balanced them on my head. For the first time it occurred to me that this might not end well.

It must have been pouring with rain farther upstream, because the water was moving faster and faster. I could feel its force against the vehicle. *What if Rover and I get washed away?* I thought. A few minutes earlier I'd been hoping that the mud would release its grip on the tire, but now I prayed that the mud would act like cement!

The water continued to pour in, and very soon I was sitting in a pool up to my waist. I knew I had to make a decision: stay in the vehicle and risk being carried off with the raging river, or crawl out the window and get to the other side. Of course, that was risky too: the current was really strong.

It dawned on me that I might actually drown. I waited expectantly for my life to flash before my eyes, but that's not what happened. I felt quite calm, and was surprised when the thought that did come to mind was simply this: *I'm happy.*

Throughout my life I'd lived thousands and thousands of happy moments, but this was unlike anything I'd felt before. It was something that came from within, not something that depended on outside events or other people. I was happy with myself, and realized how in love I was with my own life.

I certainly didn't want to die. There was still a lot of life to be lived. But if this was, in fact, the end, it was okay. I'd had so many incredible experiences, and I'd finally had the one I deemed the most important of them all: I had loved and been loved unconditionally. That was enough.

In that beautiful Zen moment, my inner smartass kicked in. *This story will make for great reading in the obituary column,* I thought. *It's been such an interesting life, it would be a shame to have a boring death.*

With the water at chest height, I decided to drop my bag and camera, and crawl out the window to make a swim for it.

Suddenly, I was surprised by the sound of a horn. I looked in the rearview mirror and saw a truck on the embankment behind me.

A work crew from a company called Tshukudu Decking had also been caught by surprise by the flash flood. Heading out to install a deck at one of the lodges, they'd left town as I had, assuming the rain hadn't started yet.

I leaned out the window. "Help?" I asked expectantly.

Immediately, two big men waded into the water and came to my aid. Another put out a call for assistance on the two-way radio. Within minutes, I was safely on shore, and vehicles from nearby lodges had come to pull the Land Rover out of the water. Before long, they had Rover on terra firma. We opened the doors and the water came gushing out.

One of my rescuers was Martin, the manager of neighbouring Rock Fig Camp. He quickly assessed the situation and determined that the only thing to do was try to dry out the vehicle. Then we'd have to wait for the water to recede so a flatbed truck could make the crossing, and Rover could be loaded up and taken to a mechanic.

Martin kindly offered to look after the Land Rover until then, opening the doors so it could dry out during the day, and closing them at night so animals wouldn't get in.

I was a grateful but shaken, soggy mess by the time I was dropped off at Tanda Tula.

Classes would have to wait for another day. The immediate issue was how I would get Susan, Ian and Spencer back to Hoedspruit now that Rover was out of commission. That problem was quickly solved, and we joined the Tanda Tula rangers who were transporting all departing guests and their luggage in the game-drive vehicles. They drove us farther north to King's Camp, which still had access to the main road. From there, shuttles from town were able to fetch all the stranded passengers.

An hour later we were in Hoedspruit — and so was the rain. I was faced with having to entertain my guests for another three days in lousy weather and with no vehicle.

That was bad, but I was absolutely dreading having to tell Johann about what had happened to his precious Land Rover. I decided to put that off for a bit and focus on the matter at hand.

It took only one phonecall to solve the transportation issue. Alicia was more than happy to help out, and it also gave her an opportunity to play tourist and visit some of the attractions she hadn't been to yet.

That left only the question of how to get the family and their luggage to Lydenburg, a town a few hours' drive away, where they were to rendezvous with someone who would take them south to Jozi and then on to KwaZulu-Natal, the next stop on their tour. Alicia's small car wasn't up to the task, so I booked them on a shuttle that would take them to Johannesburg.

There was only one phonecall left to make. As much as I wanted to, I couldn't put it off any longer. I had to call Johann. I picked up my cellphone, then put it back down. I paced back and forth, trying to decide the best way to deliver the news. I'd come to believe that every situation has a positive aspect, so I tried to look for that.

Eventually, I picked up the phone and made the call, half hoping that the signal would let us down, as it so often did. No such luck! The call went through immediately and the phone started to ring. I heard Johann's surprised voice on the other end — I rarely called him, preferring to let him call when he wasn't busy and had some privacy to talk.

"Hello, my love!" he exclaimed.

"Hello, my Rafiki," I replied, using his nickname, the Swahili word for "friend". I'd picked that up from watching *The Lion King*. He called me Nala, also from the movie; I wondered if he'd still consider me his "gift" after what I'd done to his Land Rover.

He must have heard the stress in my voice and immediately asked, "Is everything okay?"

"Well, the good news is that I didn't drown," I announced, trying to sound lighthearted.

There was a pause, then Johann said, "Hold on a second. I think I need to sit down for this."

Once the initial shock of the news had passed, my very pragmatic husband asked about the prognosis for his beloved vehicle. "So I guess it's a write-off?" he asked rhetorically.

"Not necessarily. At least I did one thing right. I couldn't decide whether or not to turn off the engine, but eventually I did turn it off. Apparently, that was the right choice and it might have saved the engine. We won't know until we get it back to town and someone can take a look at it. In the meantime, Martin from Rock Fig has the key and is going to look after drying it out for us."

"That's really good of him," replied Johann. "There's nothing we can do now. We'll just have to wait and see."

The next day I got a call from my rescuer. "Do you happen to have a spare key for the Land Rover?" Martin asked.

"I think so. Why?"

"Well, you know the guy from Umlani Lodge who also came to help pull you out yesterday? Today, he tried to make the crossing and also got stuck! I waded into the river to help him, and the current was pretty strong. Guess what was in my pocket and was carried downstream?"

"I'm guessing my key?"

"You guess right," he confirmed.

I actually took some comfort in that turn of events — not that the key had been lost, but that someone far more experienced than I in the hazards of the rainy season had made the same mistake, even with the benefit of having seen what had happened to me the day before.

I looked around for another key but couldn't find it. I had to call Johann again.

"Love, we do have a spare key, right?" I asked tentatively.

"Yeah, we have one, but it doesn't work. The remote won't open the doors, and the key won't turn in the ignition. I've been meaning to do something about that. Why?"

I explained the latest wrinkle in our predicament. We decided to send the key to the mechanics to see if they could do anything to get it to work. Until we could get the key to function, the vehicle would be sitting out in the bush with all the windows down because Martin was no longer able to close them. I tried not to think about what creatures might decide to move in and what they would do to the upholstery while we awaited Rover's rescue.

In fact, I decided to stop thinking altogether about what might happen, and to focus instead on what was actually happening. I still had my guests to consider, and I wanted to make sure they had the best time possible.

The next three days passed quite well, weather notwithstanding, and then it was time to take Susan, Ian and Spencer to catch the shuttle to Johannesburg. Again, Alicia graciously supplied a lift. The shuttle was only a few blocks from my place, so family, luggage and I managed to cram into her car for that short distance.

Despite all the drama on my side, they said they'd had a wonderful time and were falling in love with South Africa, exactly as I'd hoped they would.

Alicia and I waved a cheerful goodbye to the family as the shuttle left the parking lot. As soon as it was out of sight, I burst into tears. I was taken completely by surprise by my meltdown, but Alicia wasn't.

"I'm actually surprised you held it together as long as you did," she said, in an effort to comfort me. "Any news about the car?"

"No, it's still stuck out there, waiting for the mechanics to go and get it. I've been told not to start it for fear of buggering up the engine, if it isn't buggered up already. I wish I knew if it was going to be okay but my crystal ball doesn't seem to be working."

The days dragged on and I waited for news.

Then I got a call I wasn't expecting. It was Nina. The water level had dropped, she said, and she and Don had been on their way out to Tanda Tula when they came across the Land Rover and saw the state it was in. While Martin had been faithfully checking on it every day, there was nothing he could do about protecting it other than putting some thorny branches around it. It seemed to have stopped animals from moving in, but it hadn't deterred the hyenas, who had discovered what appeared to them to be one big chew toy! They'd gnawed on the tires, shredded and eaten the cover of the spare tire, and started chewing on the front grill, which was now missing a big chunk. The tooth marks that had been left behind were quite impressive. I'd learned on my nature-guide course that hyenas were the animals with the strongest jaws and this was certainly proof.

I thought about my husband, who got annoyed when thorns from the acacia trees scratched Rover's paint job as we drove through the bush, and wondered how he was going to react to this. I'd have to find a way to convince him that these wounds would give Rover some character and a certain rugged appeal.

The next day a flatbed truck was finally able to make its way through the muddy riverbed and Rover was loaded up and brought back to town.

The engine was checked and deemed safe to start. By some miracle, the only damage was to the water pump. The irony wasn't lost on me.

I was relieved to hear that the engine was sound plus that the electrical system had remained intact.

Rover had made it through, a little worse for wear but with no permanent damage, much like its driver. I liked to think that I'd developed a little character and some rugged appeal too!

Hyenas were here! Rover shows signs of having been snacked on

Chapter 6

It was a lazy afternoon, and all was right in my world. Johann had finished his contract in Mozambique a few months before and was home for good — or at least for now. We were really enjoying what we knew was the luxury of being home together. We were cuddled up on the couch watching a movie and contemplating lighting the fire outside.

Johann made the best potjies — traditional stews cooked in a cast-iron pot. A true potjie is never stirred. Each ingredient — whatever meat you're using, potatoes and other vegetables, spices and seasonings — is added in a layer, according to the time it takes to cook. Although Johann sometimes used the stove-top for expediency, there was nothing better than the taste of a stew that had been slowly cooked for hours over the fire. Today's selection was my favourite: chicken, ginger and coconut.

My cellphone rang. This wasn't unusual on a Sunday, as that's the day my mother normally called. I cheerfully answered, expecting to get all the latest news from home. I was surprised to hear Nina's voice and it was anything but cheerful.

"Jax, I have some bad news. Our Jeffrey was involved in a terrible car accident."

"Is he going to be okay?"

"He didn't make it, my angel. He's gone."

"Oh my God! I can't believe it! I just saw him on Thursday when he was leaving camp for his week off," I exclaimed.

I could clearly picture the moment that would prove to be the last time I would ever see that beautiful young man. He was smiling as always. I said, "Have a great time, and I'll see you when you get back."

"For sure," was his reply.

As I remembered that encounter, an indisputable truth hit home in a way it never had before: nothing is ever for sure.

"When is the funeral?" I asked.

"We don't know the plans yet. I'll let you know."

Jeffrey had been a member of the Tanda Tula family for a dozen years, working his way up from being a waiter to becoming one of the camp's star trackers. He was clever, eager and charming, and he'd set his sights on another promotion — he wanted to be a guide. Nina and Don knew he had what it would take to attain his goal, so they'd sponsored him for the nature-guide course at the Southern African Wildlife College.

He'd passed with flying colours and had continued his duties as a tracker, filling in on occasion as a guide while he waited for a fulltime guiding position to open up.

When my mom and my elder sister Michele had come to visit Johann and me the year before, we'd arranged for a game drive at Tanda Tula, and Jeffrey was our guide. Just a few minutes after we set out on our safari, he spotted tracks and drag marks in the sand. He got out of the vehicle to take a better look. "Leopard," he concluded. "Judging by the tracks, a female, dragging a kill and heading over to the riverbed."

I could hardly believe our luck. Of the "big five" — lion, leopard, elephant, rhino and buffalo — the leopard is the most elusive, solitary and secretive. And the tracks and drag marks were fresh, which meant we might be lucky enough to find where she'd settled down to feast.

Jeffrey and our tracker Sipho left the vehicle on foot, following the prints in the sand. They were gone for about ten minutes, and returned bursting with excitement.

"We found her!" Jeff proclaimed.

The cat had crossed the dry riverbed, so we drove to the other side too. The tracks led straight to a clump of bushes, with the additional cover of a fallen tree. We strained to look through the greenery to catch a glimpse of the huntress hunkered down over her prey.

Jeffrey saw it first. "She has a cub!" he exclaimed, trying to keep his voice at a whisper.

It took a moment for the rest of us to find the spots concealed between the branches of the fallen tree, but sure enough, there was the mom with her little one. They were enthusiastically making short work of the small impala the mother had killed and dragged to the spot where she'd hidden her babe. We were absolutely thrilled. And talk about beginners' luck! On my mother and sister's first-ever game drive, they'd had one of the rarest sightings — a leopard with a cub, right off the bat!

We sat and listened to the chewing and tearing for a while, then it got quiet. It seemed they'd had their fill. They lay there for a few minutes and we all strained to get a better look at the blue-eyed baby. We assumed this would be the extent of the show because full bellies generally lead to long naps.

Suddenly, the cub scampered out of its hiding place, the mother coming out on its heels. She may have been tired from the hunt and the big meal, but the baby had decided it was playtime. The two rolled in the dirt, pawing and playfully nipping at each other. They paid us no attention at all. Once that burst of energy was spent, they went back under the branches and disappeared from view.

I'll never forget the smile on Jeffrey's face. He was beaming with pride at having provided us with such an unforgettable experience. It was hard to believe that the next time I saw that young man, so full of life and promise, he would be lying in a satin-lined box in his parents' home.

A few days later I went out to the lodge to teach. The sadness was palpable among the staff. Of course, they were all very professional, and I don't think many of the guests in camp were aware of the tragedy that had befallen the Tanda Tula family. But behind the scenes there were tears and the repetition of the completely unanswerable "why?". Why had this young man been so senselessly taken from us?

Lessons about grammar would wait for another day. Today was a day to talk and to console each other. For some, talking was just too painful, so they opted to try to write about their feelings. Others, who would be working and unable to attend the funeral, wrote letters of condolence to be delivered to Jeffrey's young widow, Tracey. They grieved for their friend and despaired for those he'd left behind, including his wife and young daughter.

It had been a tough day emotionally, and after classes I set out on the winding dirt road out of the camp at a pace even slower than the fifty-kilometres-per-hour speed limit. I hoped some beautiful animals would make an appearance to brighten my mood. None did, though, all wisely staying hidden in the bush to avoid the relentless noonday sun.

I saw some movement under a tree up ahead, but soon realized that it wasn't an animal, but a young man standing in the shade. As I approached, he smiled and waved. I pulled up and asked if he needed a lift.

"Yes please, madam," he said. "I'm a tracker at Simbavati Lodge, and I'm going home on leave. Could you give me a ride to the main road?"

"Sure," I said. "Hop in."

As we carried on the down the road, we began to chat. His name was Hermet. He talked about his job as a tracker and what a thrill it gave him to show his guests all the big game, especially the cats. "You know, the overseas people are funny sometimes. You show them everything, the big five plus the wild dogs, and then they tip you fifty rand [about three US dollars]. But I don't care. It's fifty rand more than I had before. And I love to show them."

"I'm just down the road from you at Tanda Tula. I'm helping to teach the staff to read and write," I said.

"Sho!" he exclaimed. "The lodge does that for the workers?" He was clearly impressed.

By then we were passing through the main control gate, where he seemed a bit surprised by my friendly interaction with Orance, one of the guards. Farther down the road, as we approached the next gate, I slowed down and pulled over.

"Why are you stopping?" he asked. "It's your turn to go through."

"I know," I replied, "but Evans has to go get his cup so I can pour some water into it. These guys stand here all day in the hot sun, and there's no water in the guardhouse, so I always fill up my bottle before I leave camp and give the guard a drink on my way out."

A look of genuine surprise crossed his face. He seemed to be trying to make sense of what I'd just told him. Suddenly, he reached a conclusion. He turned to face me and declared, "You like black people!"

"Um... I like people," I offered.

"Many white people don't like black people," he said.

"And many black people don't like white people," I countered.

He was silent for a moment. "You said you're at Tanda Tula. Did you know Jeffrey?"

"I did," I replied, feeling a pang of sadness at my use of the past tense. "I'm waiting to hear when the funeral will be."

"You will go?" he asked.

"Of course. He was my friend."

"You really do like black people," he concluded.

"I like *people*," I repeated gently.

We'd reached the main road, and I pulled over to let him out. From there he'd either hitchhike or flag down one of the minibus taxis that made the trip out to the neighbouring village of Acornhoek and the surrounding areas.

As he was getting out of the car, he paused, then turned to ask me a question: "Do you have an African name?"

"Does 'Leopard Lady' count?" I asked. "I really like that name."

"No, I mean a proper African name. I'd like to give you one. I think your name is Tintswalo. Do you know what that means?"

"I don't," I confessed. "I just know it's the name of the hospital in Acornhoek where our friend Wendy is a doctor."

"It means 'grace'," he said. "Your African name is Grace."

138

A few days later, Nina and Don picked me up early in the morning to take me with them to Jeffrey's funeral.

The large tent that had been erected on the front lawn of Jeffrey's parents home near Acornhoek couldn't possibly accommodate all the people who'd come. The mourners spilled out on to the neighbour's lawn and on to the dirt road. Hundreds of people were there to pay their respects and to mourn with Jeffrey's family.

It had been a very long night. The funeral ceremonies had begun the evening before with a vigil that had lasted the entire night. The funeral service had started at first light.

When we arrived, we were ushered to the front seats in the tent. Those already sitting there made way for us, the honoured guests. I felt humbled and more than a little embarrassed that people who were close to the family and had been mourning all night were being relocated to make room for us, the new arrivals and the only white faces in the crowd. I'd been told to expect this; the presence of Don and Nina as the owners of the lodge was a high tribute to Jeffrey and was viewed as a great honour for his family. While I felt incredibly uncomfortable, I comforted myself with the thought that in some small way my presence might make the family feel even the slightest bit better.

I was seated near Jeff's widow, Tracey. I'd had the pleasure of working with her at Tanda Tula a few times, when we were both recruited to entertain private groups at Tandala, a smaller lodge on the property that was occasionally used for private parties. We'd worked together well, and had really enjoyed each other's company. She was cheerful and intelligent, and had a great sense of humour.

Now, the woman I'd always thought of as a bundle of joy and energy was nearly unrecognizable. She was completely overwhelmed by grief. I can only describe her as being shattered. She sat on the ground, rocking back and forth, sobbing, seemingly oblivious to everything except her despair.

When the service was over, Tracey was helped to her feet by her sister and led out of the tent. The entire funeral party followed. We all had to make our way down the dusty, bumpy road to the burial site. Nina, Don and I set off with as many of the Tanda Tula staff as we could squeeze into their Land Rover. Many other mourners crammed into smaller cars and filled the cargo areas of small pick-up trucks, or bakkies, as they're called in South Africa. Those who couldn't find a lift walked the considerable distance to the graveyard.

When we reached our destination Nina, Don and I found ourselves once again being escorted to a place of honour. We were sitting in the front row of chairs under the marquee that had been erected at the graveside.

Now Tracey was sitting right at my feet, her body still swaying to the rhythm of her mostly silent sobbing. She used a hand towel to catch the endless stream of tears, saliva and snot that no number of tissues could have withstood. I put my hand on her shoulder and gently rubbed her back, but I'm not sure she even knew I was there.

Her sister clung to her, sobbing even harder. She seemed to be mourning not just the loss of Jeffrey but also the devastating impact that his death was having on the sister she so clearly loved. I kept rubbing Tracey's back, hoping that somehow she would feel even a little comfort from this small, entirely inadequate gesture.

Once the ceremony was over, Tracey was once again helped to her feet by her sister and other female relatives. Those who had rides drove, while the remainder of the funeral party began the long walk back to the family's home where a meal would be served.

Jeffrey's Tanda Tula family was asked to stay behind for final prayers and the actual burial. We encircled the grave and said our last goodbyes.

With the formalities of the ceremonies completed, we made our way back to the house. As we approached, I could tell there had been a radical shift in the mood of the crowd.

At the entrance to the front yard, a man with a tree branch dipped its leaves into a bucket of holy water and splashed each of us in turn.

"What's that about?" I asked Clenny, who'd come to meet me as I came through the gate.

"It's to wash away the sadness of the funeral," she explained.

I was surprised to feel my sadness start to lift, and as I looked around I could see other people were smiling. The ritual had done its job, and the mood of the gathering shifted from sombre remembrance to a celebration of Jeffrey's life.

Soon it was time to serve the food, and though there were hundreds of people there before us, Nina, Don and I were once again treated like dignitaries and taken to the front of the line. I felt uneasy and embarrassed being served first, but was reassured by the smiles and hugs of my friends and co-workers. They were truly grateful for our presence.

The next time I went out to Tanda Tula to teach, I could tell that my relationship with the staff had shifted to a new level. I'd always felt their affection and respect, but it seemed now that their trust had deepened. They all thanked me for having attended the funeral.

That evening I was in the bar with Smiling, awaiting the return of the guests after the game drive. "You did really good, you know, and we really appreciate it," he said.

"But Smiling, I didn't do anything," I said. "All I did was show up."

"You cared enough to show up," he responded. "That's all you had to do."

The leopard and cub Jeffrey and Sipho tracked on our game drive

Enjoying the sunset: Michele, Jeffrey, Mom, Sipho and Johann

Chapter 7

"Warning: Poachers Will Be Poached!"

This is what the huge black, red and white billboards proclaim as you enter our little town via any of the three tarred roads that lead to Hoedspruit. We're at the centre of the largest rhino population in South Africa, which means we're also ground zero for the poachers who are determined to cut off their horns. The big signs are sponsored by an organization called Rhino Revolution, and while I emphatically support their cause, I wish they'd change that slogan. It seems to me that the "eye for an eye" mentality only leads to mass blindness.

It's easy to understand their passion. The sight of a rhino that has been butchered, its face hacked off for its horn, is nothing short of horrifying. It's not difficult to see why the people who seek to protect the animals, the chopper pilots and rangers who're faced with seeing this atrocity over and over again, would be out for blood.

But the issue of the poaching of rhinos, elephants, lions and other vulnerable species isn't that simple. The poacher they're threatening to poach could be part of a crime syndicate, but chances are he's a man from a small village who's trying to feed his family. He's been offered more money than he ever dreamed of to go into the Kruger National Park or one of the private game reserves in the area to slaughter a rhino and bring back its horn. It's a useless piece of keratin, the same stuff our fingernails are made of, but because of a combination of traditional beliefs and modern misinformation, it fetches a ridiculous price in certain markets. Per gram, rhino horn is more valuable in many Far Eastern countries than diamonds, platinum or cocaine.

A few years ago a very public figure in Vietnam declared that rhino horn could prevent cancer. It's also been touted as a cure for hangovers and an aphrodisiac. Some believe that consuming the horn will give them the strength of the rhino. And because of its high price, having rhino horn is considered a status symbol. There are even speculators coming into the market, hoarding the horn, believing that it will become even more valuable when the animal is extinct.

Does the man determined to kill this magnificent beast know that these creatures have roamed the earth for nearly fifty million years, and that they could be extinct within the next twenty? Would it make a difference if he did? Maybe, maybe not. What he does know is that, as lucrative as it is, poaching is extremely risky.

He knows there are armed patrols and tracking dogs out looking for him and those like him. He'll slip on to the property and look for a place to hide — maybe an abandoned aardvark or warthog burrow. He'll wait for the cover of darkness, then track his prey. Once he's found it, he'll shoot it, hack off its horn, and make his way out of the park as fast as he can.

He'll hand over the horn to the middleman who hired him and he'll get paid. It'll be more money than he's ever seen in his life, but it will be a pittance compared to what the horn will fetch on the black market. The middleman makes a bundle, and the kingpin makes a killing.

What happens if we do, in fact, "poach the poacher"? A desperately poor family loses their father and becomes even more desperate. And there are hundreds more equally desperate men ready to take the dead man's place and try their luck at making a fortune.

It seems to me that the only solution is to make the horn worthless. That's been attempted by injecting it with dye or even poison, so that it can't be consumed. The injections seemed like a brilliant solution, but sadly they didn't work. The poachers would spend hours tracking a rhino, and then, on discovering that the horn had been tainted, would shoot the animal anyway, making sure that they wouldn't waste more precious time tracking the same animal again later.

Dehorning had the same effect: the poachers would steal the stub that was left and leave the corpse to rot.

And the matter of the corpses was another issue — vultures would circle them, alerting the anti-poaching teams to the location of the kill, and putting them hot on the heels of the poacher. To prevent this, many poachers had taken to poisoning the corpses, which killed the vultures that fed on them. This, along with several other factors such as habitat loss, electrocution on power lines and the use of vulture parts in traditional medicine, has contributed to the massive decline in vulture numbers. Many species of vultures are endangered.

While the spotlight and fundraising were firmly focused on the plight of rhinos, the danger to elephants was escalating, and was by all accounts about to get worse. In the 1970s and '80s there had been an elephant-poaching crisis, but the international community came together to ban the ivory trade and the elephant population recovered in the '90s.

Then, in the early 2000s, the rise of the middle class in China fuelled the price of ivory on the black market as more and more people were prepared to pay top dollar for what they considered a luxury or status product. The illegal trade in ivory experienced a boom, and the industry, run by gangs and organized crime, is now worth billions.

In 2016 statistics showed that ninety-six elephants a day were being slaughtered across Africa. At that rate, elephants could become extinct in the next few decades.

Thankfully, the international community seemed to be paying attention and responding at a grassroots level. The Global March for Elephants and Rhinos was born.

I was listening to a Johannesburg radio station when I heard about the event, and I got very excited. I loved the idea of people all over the world coming together to march in support of our precious wildlife. I grabbed my computer and quickly googled the event to find a list of locations. Some of the bigger centres in South Africa were listed, but Hoedspruit wasn't.

With only two weeks until the event took place, I had to act fast. Luckily, I knew exactly who could make this happen in a hurry. Tracy and I had become great friends since our *House Hunters International* shoot, and if anyone had the contacts, the energy and the drive to get the job done, she was the one.

Without hesitation, she jumped in and started organizing immediately. Within days, our march was on — and it was going to be spectacular!

It would take place on the grounds of one of the premier wildlife estates in town, Zandspruit Bush and Aero Estate. Our group would get to march across a dry riverbed and through a wilderness area where we might encounter zebras, giraffes and wildebeest. We also created a shorter, wheelchair-friendly route so everyone could be included. We wanted everyone to be there.

In less than a week, posters were up around town and we started advertising on social media. The excitement spread quickly, and another march was announced on one of the private game reserves for those who wouldn't be able to make it into town. It was thrilling to feel the momentum building.

When the day arrived, Johann and I were up very early, eager and ready. When we arrived at the Zandspruit gate to help with the setup, Tracy and the other volunteers were already in full swing and the energy was electric. We were all excited, and we couldn't wait to see how many people would come.

We didn't have long to wait. The early birds soon started to arrive: teams from companies and schools, groups of friends, families and neighbours. As the start time drew nearer, more and more people flocked to the starting point. More than a dozen students from a local environmental protection programme, appropriately clad in green, exuberantly led the march, hoisting high and with great pride our "Global March for Elephants, Rhinos and Lions" banner. They were followed by a wonderfully diverse group of a few hundred: black and white, and ranging from toddlers to seniors, some running, a few in wheelchairs, most walking, including moms pushing babies in strollers. The mood of the crowd was positively jubilant.

As we snaked our way along the path, we heard an aeroplane approaching. Manned by a volunteer pilot and photographer, it swooped down over us, waving and taking photos. The crowd responded, cheering and waving excitedly.

As I marched along, I felt a pure positive energy and on a deep level realized the reason it was being created: we were marching *for* elephants and rhinos, not *against* poachers. I'd been working with that concept for quite some time, but I'd never understood it with such clarity or felt the truth of it more profoundly.

The principle is simple — what you focus on expands in your experience, whether it's wanted or unwanted. It's not difficult to find examples of this. For years we've been hearing about the various "wars" mankind has been waging. There's a war on drugs, a war on poverty and a war on terror. Instead of being solved, all of these issues are getting bigger. The negative focus increases resistance, and what you resist, persists.

The Global March for Elephants and Rhinos took a completely different approach: we were standing up for the animals, not railing against the poachers. I was sure that with all the positive focus we were generating regarding rhinos and elephants, they were about to come into my experience big time!

By the time we'd finished the march and had all gathered back at the main gate for refreshments and speeches, I was feeling nothing short of euphoric. I was already anticipating my drive out to Tanda Tula the next day and the amazing encounters I was sure were in store for me.

I got up at the crack of dawn. Anticipating all the great photos I'd soon be snapping, I made sure that my camera was charged and ready to go. Stowing it safely on the passenger seat, I left more than an hour earlier than usual, convinced that I'd need the extra time to spend with all the rhinos and elephants I was absolutely convinced would come out to rendezvous with me.

I pulled up to the gate of Timbavati game reserve and was greeted by Orance, who was a bit surprised to see me there much earlier than usual. I explained to him that I had a feeling that I'd need the extra time. He smiled indulgently and gave me the two-thumbs-up that means "sha'p" — a South African expression used by all races meaning "cool" or "right on".

The first creatures I encountered were monkeys — nothing unusual there. They liked to hang out on a marula tree not too far from the gate. They were always fun to watch, but this was even more special because of the number of tiny babies in the troupe.

I stopped to play one of my favourite games — "monkey see, monkey do". I picked one monkey out of the crowd and we locked eyes. I cocked my head to the left and he mirrored my action, cocking his to the right. I moved to the right; he moved to the left. I crouched down in my seat, and he immediately lowered himself. I sat up tall, and he stretched up on his toes.

This game can go on for a very long time, so after one round I ended it and carried on down the road looking for bigger game.

I knew the chances of seeing a rhino by the roadside were slim, but I had no doubt that a herd of elephants would appear at any moment. I drove slowly, scanning from right to left and back again. Soon, something big and grey caught my eye. "Rock or rhino?" I asked myself out loud. Then it moved and the answer was clear — rhino!

I pulled off to the side of the road and switched off the engine. I picked up the camera and was happily snapping shots, when another rhino wandered into the frame. I hadn't even seen him! I was once again amazed at how such large animals can become invisible behind the smallest of shrubs and trees.

I spent a good twenty minutes watching the pair, then decided to get back on my way. Surely the elephants would put in an appearance soon. There were a couple of watering holes farther along, and I'd often been treated to good sightings at both of them.

I approached the first one with anticipation. The place was completely deserted. There wasn't even a stray impala or wildebeest to be seen.

I carried on with high hopes to the next small body of water. Nothing there either.

As I drove along, I approached each bend in the road expectantly, sure that I'd run into a massive grey roadblock at any moment. No such luck.

As I crossed the riverbed, I looked left and right, straining to catch sight of any silhouettes in the distance. Nothing but trees as far as the eye could see. I'd be at camp soon, and I simply couldn't believe that I'd arrive there without having seen even a single elephant. I could've sworn that I could actually feel their presence; I just couldn't see them.

I rounded the final bend in the road, and pulled into the Tanda Tula parking lot. I'd reached my destination without seeing any elephants.

Before I allowed any disappointment to set it, I reminded myself that there was still the drive home ahead, as there wasn't room for me to stay over in the camp that night. Maybe the elephants were waiting for my return trip.

I checked my watch, and seeing that it was still early, decided to go down to the main lodge to find Harry. Like his brother Smiling, he was one of the bartenders at the camp. He was also one of my best students. He'd likely be restocking the bar while the guests were out on their morning drive. I wanted to find out what time he'd be able to come to class, and if he wanted to work on his English or continue with his French lessons. I hoped we could do both because he was so much fun to teach.

When I walked into the main lodge, the bar was empty, but the watering hole just beyond it was full... of elephants!

I stood there motionless for a moment, absolutely stunned. Then a feeling of elation and pure joy blossomed inside me.

I dropped my bag and raced through the empty bar, across the lawn and past the swimming pool. I stopped when I got as close to the water as the elephant wire — the single strand of high-voltage electric cable that prevented the elies coming into the camp — would allow me.

I'd never seen such a big, beautiful herd. They all stood in the water, and I watched as the young ones played, intertwining their trunks and pushing and pulling each other in what looked like a gentle tug of war. The adults filled their trunks, by turn emptying the water into their mouths for a drink, or spraying themselves to cool down. It felt as if I was in a dream and I struggled to comprehend that this was really happening. It was like I'd imagined it, only better!

It occurred to me that I should count the elephants — no easy task with all that playful activity. After a few false starts, I managed: there were twenty-eight.

I suddenly realized that I didn't have my camera. It didn't look like they were ready to leave, but that usually happens quite suddenly, when the matriarch decides it's time to move on. I decided to take a chance, and ran back to the Land Rover, hoping that the elephants would wait for me.

I arrived back at the dam, camera in hand, just in time to see the matriarch leave the water. Immediately, the rest of the herd followed, and so did I.

It looked like they were heading for the riverbed crossing, so I ran to the far end of the camp, where the smaller lodge, Tandala, sat at the edge of the property. I caught up with them just before they reached the crossing, and I stopped to watch as they filed past me, just metres away. All that stood between us was a thin electric wire. I could almost have reached out and touched them.

The matriarch leading the way began her crossing. I couldn't follow any more, but I knew that if I hurried, I had one last opportunity to see them. I rushed down to the deck of Tandala's master bedroom, which jutted out over the riverbank. I watched in awe as the twenty-eight trekked silently in single file across the dry sand. The lead elephants disappeared into the bush, with the rest following close behind. It never ceased to amaze me how swiftly and silently a herd could move, and how quickly they seemingly vanished.

I thought I was seeing the end of them when the last elephant in line decided to break rank. He turned around and walked straight towards me, stopping just short of the deck. He could've touched me with his trunk, and I wondered if that was his plan as I watched him slowly reach up, but he settled on a branch on the bush right beneath my perch. With great dexterity, he broke off the branch and put it into his mouth. The bush was still and quiet, with the exception of the sound of him chewing on the branch and the tender green leaves. It was one of those rare, amazing moments in life when time seems to stand still. I hoped he could sense how much I appreciated his presence.

As if in response to that thought, he let out a low rumble, to my ear one of the most beautiful sounds on earth. Elephants have an amazing repertoire of vocalizations, from ear-piercing trumpets to rumbles so low they can only be felt, not heard. I'd been told that elephants enjoy the sound of the human voice because it resembles some of their rumbling sounds. I liked to think this elephant had chosen a rumble I could hear because he was talking to me.

"Thank you," I said, keeping my pitch low in an effort to match his.

That was the extent of the conversation. He turned and wandered off to rejoin the rest of the herd.

Alicia and I unfurl the banner for the Global March for Elephants

Tracy welcomes the crowd

Twenty-eight elephants

159

Chapter 8

I'm not religious enough to be a farmer. Unfortunately, I was unaware of that fact until after the big hailstorm.

It never hailed in Hoedspruit — at least, that's what people said. Imagine our surprise, then, when our crop of six thousand granadilla plants was flattened and shredded to bits by huge chunks of ice falling from the sky.

According to a few of the local, very conservative farmers in the area, the reason our crop had been hit was due to a lack of church attendance on our part. Apparently regular attendance has its benefits, including holy hail insurance. And, as you would expect, God has really good aim. The farms around ours were unscathed.

Going into the granadilla business had seemed like a good idea at the time. From the research we'd done, the crop was a good choice for Hoedspruit. With our year-round warm, hail-free (ha!) climate, the plants would thrive. We'd have fruit on our vines for most of the year, while in other parts of the country they'd produce only one harvest. With that advantage, surely we'd have fruit when others didn't, and the decrease in supply would boost the price at the Jozi market?

If only things had gone according to plan.

The surprise hailstorm wasn't the only setback recently suffered on the little farm Rob and Alicia had rented outside of town. The last crop of baby marrows and pattypan squash they'd been getting ready to harvest had been hit by a virus. The whole lot was ruined and had to be burned.

It wasn't the first time it had happened, which was one of the reasons they'd wanted to plant granadillas — they were much sturdier plants.

Discouraged by yet another lost crop, Rob and Alicia decided not to plant baby vegetables again. That had been the first wrinkle in our master plan — the vegetables were supposed to pay the expenses for the farm while the fruit crop got up and running. Now all our money was riding on the granadillas.

Up until the freak storm, the progress of the crop had been right on track. The first three thousand plants we'd put in the ground in April were healthy and thriving; after just five months they were starting to show signs of producing fruit.

Encouraged, we decided to put more money into the business and add another block of three thousand plants in October. Because the planting times were staggered, we figured that the second block would be bearing fruit when the first block had finished. If we were lucky, we'd have a steady yield through most of the year, and recover our investment quickly. It was a great plan on paper.

On reflection, after the event, it occurred to me that the storm was a confirmation of the life lessons I'd recently learned from other painful experiences: Jeffrey's death had underlined that nothing is for sure, and my close call in the riverbed confirmed that you can't control nature.

But other events had taught me something else as well: often things that appear to be disastrous ultimately aren't, and there's a gift in almost every circumstance. I considered this to be life's greatest secret, and now that I knew it, I'd have to put it into practice.

So, instead of panicking and being devastated by the freak storm and the flattened plants, I chose to believe that things were working out for us. I tried to imagine how that might unfold, and I settled on this: maybe because the plants had had a major pruning, when they did eventually bear fruit, it would be bigger and sweeter, and the crop more bountiful.

It wasn't long after the hailstorm that I received a heartwarming and genuinely uplifting message. It had been four years since I'd been in South Sudan, where I'd travelled on an aid trip with Canadian Aid for South Sudan. I'd still occasionally hear from some of the boys I'd met when I was helping out at the art-and-music camp. They didn't readily have computer access, but when they did manage to get online, they'd always reach out to their Canadian friends.

Their messages always touched me. They used phrases that first-language English speakers would never use and the effect was often quite poetic. David was one of the first people I'd met when I'd arrived in the village of Gordhim, and he held a special place in my heart. When he'd written to me last, he'd said, "I have found myself at a computer and I am taking this golden moment of opportunity to speak with you my dear friend." That had made me smile.

But the message I received from Butrus actually brought tears of joy. When I'd met him in 2010, Butrus was 17 years old and was just finishing elementary school. Years of conflict in the region had forced schooling to be suspended for a period of about five years. While Canadian Aid for South Sudan had been working diligently to get a high school built in the area, the completion of that project was at that time still several years away. Understandably, Butrus hadn't wanted to wait. He'd already lost so much time.

I'd agreed to help him with the money he needed for travel, school fees, and room and board at a school in faraway Juba. With the help of my family and friends, we'd sponsored him for the required four years. I couldn't wait to share with them the message Butrus had sent.

"My unforgotten friend," the email read. "Bravo to you dear, for you have lifted me and pulled me out of the darkness. I completed my senior [subjects] last year with good result. Because of your help now I can swim in the ocean with the other swimmers. I am fine indeed. I look forward to hear from you. May my hugs always be with you. Thanks a lot sweet friend."

Butrus had successfully finished high school!

At about the same time I received that message, I learned that the high school Canadian Aid for South Sudan had envisioned in the area would soon be open. Finally, education would be available to everyone, not just those who were fortunate enough to find sponsors.

Our granadillas may not have been flourishing, but I took great comfort in knowing that the seeds planted several years ago in South Sudan were coming to glorious fruition.

Meanwhile, at Raptors' Lodge, another long-held dream was about to come true. We were about to welcome a new resident. Our peacock friend Paulus was finally going to meet his match.

The lonely bird had been wandering around the property for months, forlornly displaying his impressive tail feathers, but still had found no takers. Finally, one of the Raptors' Lodge residents, Hoedspruit's beloved veterinarian, Pete, took pity on the poor guy. Pete managed to locate a solitary peahen in a nearby village and would be bringing her home to meet our bachelor bird. It was decided that her name would be Penelope, and we were all excited to see Paulus's reaction when she arrived.

In bringing the two together, we'd hoped for chemistry, but what we got instead was physics: his every action brought an equal and opposite reaction from his intended. He came forward; she backed away. He stood in front of her, fanning his magnificent tail feathers; she turned her back to him. He manoeuvred himself in front of her again; once more, she turned away.

This was clearly going to take persistence, patience and time — the three things required to accomplish virtually anything in Africa.

Nowhere was this more apparent than in our dealings with the Department of Home Affairs. To live in South Africa with my husband, I had to apply for a Relative's Permit every two years. This was never as simple as it sounded.

I'd made my first application shortly after our marriage, when we were living in a town called Kroonstad in Free State province. We'd had to travel to the nearest office, about sixty kilometres away in the larger town of Welkom. *Surely that had to be a good sign?* I'd thought — *I would be made welcome in Welkom.* When I mentioned this to my husband, his response was a raised eyebrow and a wry smile.

With the help of instructions downloaded from the internet, we located the Department of Homes Affairs office and easily found a parking space. I marvelled at our good luck — which promptly ran out.

The queue to get to the service counter started at the door. There were at least ten people ahead of us waiting to take a place in the dozen rows of metal chairs that filled the large waiting area.

Eventually, the last seats in the back row opened up as the occupants of the first seats in the first row were finally summoned to the counter.

The hours crept by, as we ever so slowly moved up seat by seat, row by row, towards the windows at the counter which were sporadically manned by civil servants. Where they disappeared to or why, we had no idea. The absences went well beyond what you'd expect for tea breaks.

We'd arrived at 9am, and the lunch hour was well underway by the time we reached what we estimated to be the halfway mark. Johann was frustrated and I was getting anxious — would we make it to the counter before the office closed for the day?

As closing time crept closer, the queue inched along as each person moved into the seat vacated by the person ahead of them. With only half an hour left of the working day, we were in the front row; and, finally, with just minutes to spare, it was our turn to be called to the counter.

A wave of relief washed over me as I handed the man my paperwork, which he promptly rejected.

Because I was applying for an extended visa, I had to submit a medical and radiology report, including a chest X-ray to check for tuberculosis. For some reason, the man behind the counter wasn't happy with my chest X-ray from Canada. I'd have to get another and try again another day. I feared that with all the chest X-rays needed, I'd glow in the dark by the time we'd been married for the five years required before I could finally apply for permanent residence!

The second time I'd had to apply, we'd moved to Hoedspruit. The nearest office was about a hundred kilometres away, in the town of Phalaborwa.

After signing in at the main office, we were directed to the permits office, which we were delighted to see had no queue at all. The door was slightly ajar, and I knocked gently as I tentatively peered in.

The official sat behind her desk, deep in conversation with the cleaning lady, who was seated on the other side in what was presumably a client's chair. Both were obviously annoyed by the interruption.

"Excuse me," I ventured. "I'd like to apply for a Relative's Permit."

The cleaning lady got up, but rather than leave the room, she grabbed another chair and firmly planted herself in it, next to her boss; apparently, she'd decided to sit in on our meeting.

Johann and I settled into the clients' chairs and offered up the paperwork we'd downloaded from the internet and carefully prepared.

Barely glancing at it, the official threw it back down in front of us. "No good," she said.

"Why?" I asked incredulously.

"You left the country," came her terse reply. "You went back to Canada."

Reaching into one of the desk drawers, she pulled out another set of forms. She fished around and found another piece of paper, then circled several items on a long list. "Get all these things, fill in those forms and come back."

I looked at the circled items in disbelief. *Another* chest X-ray? It seemed absolutely unnecessary, but at least I could get that. But a police clearance from Canada? That would be next to impossible in the amount of time I had before my current permit expired.

"Honestly, I went home to be with my mother while she was going through breast cancer. I didn't go home to get TB and commit crimes!"

"Get all these things, fill in those forms and come back," the official repeated dispassionately.

I fought back tears of righteous indignation and despair as we left the office.

"Have a great day further," she called out after me.

Normally, that direct English translation of the Afrikaans equivalent of "Have a good day" made me smile — to me, it implied that up until that point you'd already been having a great day. That was obviously not the case that day, and I wasn't sure if in this instance the remark was said out of habit or sarcasm.

Johann and I went to a nearby clinic and I had the X-ray done, but there was no technician there at the time who could read it and fill in the report: we'd have to come back and get it in a week's time.

At first I was terribly upset, but then I had a moment of clarity. For a few years I'd been playing with the idea of living unconditionally, and here was the perfect time to put it into practice. The official at Home Affairs and the requirements she'd demanded were just conditions. I didn't have to let those conditions determine how I felt. I could decide how to feel.

I made the decision to change my mind, and not label the requirements as unreasonable or impossible. In fact, I didn't have to label them at all. They were simply requirements.

I'd learned that in dealing with any seemingly adverse situation, the trick was to find the path of least resistance. I thought about it for a while and concluded that the path would be the long road to Nelspruit, and a different branch of Home Affairs. It would mean driving twice as far, but I knew the woman in the small town of Phalaborwa didn't want to help me. I set my intention to find someone in the much larger centre of Nelspruit who would.

The following week we drove the hour north to pick up the X-ray and report, then drove the two and a half hours south to Nelspruit.

We got to the Home Affairs office and waited in line. The line moved surprisingly quickly, and before we knew it, we were handing the paperwork to an official. I'd set my intention, and truly believed that things would work out for me.

The official looked over the forms, turned and walked away. He came back with new forms and slid them across the counter. I was dumbfounded.

"The forms they gave you in Phalaborwa aren't acceptable," he said. "They obviously ran out of forms and decided to photocopy them. Here are some original forms. Just transfer your information on to these. And you don't need to get a Canadian police clearance. Just go down the block to the police station and sign an affidavit that says you were home for a visit but that you didn't commit any crime while you were there.

"As soon as you have that, come back and see me. Don't wait in line, just come straight to my counter, and as soon as I finish with the person I'm dealing with, I'll accept your application form."

Within an hour, the new forms were filled out and my application, complete with police affidavit, was filed. What had seemed impossible a week before had been accomplished with ease.

I decided that, in future, whenever I had to think about visiting government offices or filing paperwork, I'd picture that wonderful man who'd been so helpful. And I hoped we'd meet again when it was time for me to file for my Permanent Residence permit on Johann's and my fifth wedding anniversary.

Chapter 9

What do you want to be when you grow up?

When I was a very young child, I remember that I wanted to be two things: an artist and a writer. It thrilled me now to be living part of that dream, and I was really enjoying creating images with Alicia as Two Girls and an Elephant.

And now that I'd found the courage to create art, maybe it was time to push myself even further out of my comfort zone?

When I looked back on it, I could see how what I considered to be my complete failure at art as a child had created one of my core beliefs. I was convinced that I wasn't creative. Rather than risking failure by trying my hand at creative writing, I'd decided to stick with the facts, which was how I ended up working in radio newsrooms. For me, it was a safe compromise; by writing news stories, I was writing without the risk. And while I'd managed to make a very successful career of it, and even did manage to become more creative in my role as an on-air personality rather than a newscaster, I must admit I'd never felt completely satisfied.

I'd abandoned the dream of being a writer — but I was beginning to realize that the dream hadn't abandoned me.

Since taking my huge leap of faith and moving to South Africa for love, many people had told me that I should write a book. At first I dismissed the idea — who was I to write a book? Over time, though, the idea started to resonate with me. I wanted to write, and if sharing my experiences could in some way inspire someone else who was feeling stuck in their life, then it would be worthwhile.

When we were living in Kroonstad, I certainly had enough time on hands, so I gave it a try. After several false starts I gave up on the idea, convincing myself that my writing wasn't that good and that my story wasn't really all that interesting anyway.

Several years later, I met someone who would help me change my mind.

There was considerable excitement at Tanda Tula when I arrived for my regular teaching days. A VIP guest had just checked in. Tony Park was a well-known writer in the southern hemisphere. He was from Australia, but after a bucket-list trip he'd become besotted with South Africa and now split his time between the two countries. His action-packed novels were set mostly in Africa. I immediately recognized his name from my bookshop perusing — he was a prolific writer and his many popular novels were always prominently on display.

I had no idea that he and his wife Nicola were friends of Tanda Tula owners Don and Nina. They'd invited the Parks for a few days of relaxation as their guests.

It occurred to me that I should speak to Tony about my abandoned manuscript. Then it occurred to me what a truly terrible idea that was. He was a famous novelist; he was probably constantly being hounded by would-be writers. He was here on holiday — the last thing he'd want would be for some random person to corner him and start talking about their pathetic attempts at writing.

When I met him by the pool later that afternoon, I just couldn't help myself. He was approachable, disarmingly friendly and completely down to earth. We started out chatting about the adult-literacy programme and how much I loved teaching, and I ended up telling him how I'd tried to write my story a few times, but had eventually given up on the idea.

"Tell me your story," he said.

I quickly rattled off the condensed version: losing my career, my marriage and an election, the mission trip to South Sudan where I met the love of my life, and the new life I was building for myself as a teacher and artist in South Africa.

He listened attentively, then stated simply, "It's a great story. I think you should write it."

That was all I needed to hear.

When I got home the next day, I opened up the abandoned

manuscript and started to write again. Tony's encouragement helped me to let go of my doubt, and to believe that I could actually finish the book. I also finally believed that the book was worth finishing.

My momentum was soon broken, though — by a broken hip. I got a call from my mom to tell me that Dad had fallen, and was in the hospital.

"Should I come home?" I asked

"No, it's fine. There's really nothing you can do anyway," she replied.

"Okay, but let me know if you change your mind, and keep me posted."

She called again a few days later with an update. Dad was still in the hospital, in isolation with pneumonia.

"Do you want me to come home?" I asked.

"No, we're fine."

Then there was another call a few days later: "Dad thinks maybe you should come home. He'd really like to see you. Johann too, if he can come. Then we'll all be together for Christmas."

Johann couldn't come. He'd been signed on as a medic on an Australian reality-TV show that was about to start filming in the mountains outside of town. He'd be at the location several days a week in December as a health and safety officer, and as standby medic while the set was being built. Then, in January, he'd move out to the set for the almost three months it would take for the show to be filmed.

But I quickly booked my ticket and packed my bags.

As I settled in for the long flight, I tried to decide whether I was going home or leaving home. It seemed to be both. Canada would always be home, but I realized that South Africa was now my home too.

Dad was still in the hospital when I arrived, but the doctor gave him permission to come home for the weekend. When we went to pick him up, it had been snowing all night, and the roads were snow-packed and slippery. Mom and I helped him into the car, and as we slowly drove the few kilometres home, I wondered how we'd get him into the house. I'd shovelled a path from the head of the driveway up the two stairs he'd have to climb to reach the front door, and sprinkled a good measure of salt along it to melt the ice.

When we arrived, I pulled the car up as close to the stairs as I could. Mom opened the front door as I got the walker out of the trunk, then helped Dad out of the car. So far, so good.

I stood behind him with my arm around his waist and he put the walker up on the first step. He put his right leg on the step and tried to get the left leg to follow. It seemed the connection between the brain and the leg wasn't working — and suddenly I felt him start to fall backwards.

I instinctively thrust my right knee forward and lunged to catch him under the butt. I stood in full-on yoga warrior position, with my father's dead weight precariously balanced on my knee. I couldn't summon up the strength to push him back up to a standing position, and there was no way I could gently lower him to the ground.

I couldn't think of what to do, and I struggled to hold the position.

"You okay, Dad?"

"Yeah. You?"

"Yeah. I'm just not sure for how long."

Suddenly, my dad, the walker and I were miraculously swept up in a pair of big, astonishingly strong arms. Before I knew what was happening, we were up the stairs, over the threshold and deposited safely in the house. Our neighbour, a strapping man from Newfoundland, had chanced to look out the window at just the right moment. Without hesitation, he'd rushed to our rescue.

Fortunately, the rest of the weekend unfolded with far less drama.

Once Dad had been safely delivered back to the hospital on the Monday morning, I had some business to attend to. Johann's and my fifth wedding anniversary was fast approaching, and I'd finally be able to become a permanent resident of South Africa. At last I'd have the legal right to work in my adopted country. While I understood that the five-year waiting period was designed to protect the jobs of South Africans, it had been a very long time for a forced "time out" in my career.

As you'd expect, the dates of the expiry of my Relative's Permit and our fifth anniversary didn't match up, so I'd have to re-apply for my Relative's Permit in May, and then file for permanent residence in July.

In the meantime, my unexpected trip home meant that I could apply for my Canadian police clearance in person. I filled out the paperwork at the local police station and asked that it not be submitted until February so that its six-month validity period would cover both the applications I had to make. I requested two copies of the document, and would have them couriered to South Africa in plenty of time. I was feeling quite pleased with myself for being so organized.

Soon Dad was released from the hospital and my sisters both came home for Christmas. I missed Johann, but I really was mastering the art of enjoying all that was good in the present moment and not focusing on what was missing. I enjoyed having another white Christmas with my family and friends in Canada, knowing I'd get back to my other home in Hoedspruit in time to ring in the New Year with my husband.

On 2 January Johann reported for work fulltime on the set of the Australian version of *I'm a Celebrity, Get Me Out of Here*. The location the contestants thought was in the middle of the "jungle" (we never could get them to call it the bush) was in fact only about thirty kilometres outside of town, close to our old place at Ver End. Johann would be living out there for the next two and a half months, but he would get to come home one night a week. While I wasn't looking forward to yet another separation, I was glad he'd found an interesting job and that there would be some money coming in. I was also excited to get back to teaching classes at Tanda Tula and was eager to dedicate myself to finally finishing my manuscript.

Only one of those things happened. My time at Tanda Tula unexpectedly came to an abrupt end. As the lodge had become more successful and ever busier, it had also become harder for the staff to find time to come to classes. Now that many had a solid foundation for literacy, they would be able to carry on independently. The number of classes had been cut and could easily be handled by one teacher, so I was no longer needed. As a business decision it made perfect sense. From my personal perspective, it was utterly devastating.

I'd loved every minute of the nearly three years I'd been a part of that very special family and that amazing place. I'd absolutely revelled in being there. I loved teaching and I was good at it. It had thrilled me to see my friends gain new skills and self-confidence. I'd loved meeting all the wonderful guests from all over the world. I'd never missed an opportunity to go out on a game drive and learn from some of the best trackers and guides on the continent. I'd enjoyed contributing to the blog, and had amassed thousands of amazing photographs. It had been an extraordinary experience, and, given the choice, I would've stayed forever.

Now the choice had been made for me.

There's a quote attributed to the Buddha that says, "In the end only three things matter: how much you loved, how gently you lived and how gracefully you let go of things not meant for you." I knew I was doing well on the first two points, but the news that I was no longer part of the adult-literacy programme let me know that I had a long way to go regarding the third. I couldn't imagine my life in South Africa without being a part of Tanda Tula.

Despite my understanding that pain is inevitable but suffering is a choice, I lingered in the place of suffering over my perceived loss for far longer than I care to admit. I was heartbroken, and it hurt like hell.

But, as Winston Churchill so famously said, "If you're going through hell, keep going."

I had to let go of resisting the situation and accept that, once again, life was moving me along. I had to trust that this ultimately would lead to something better. When life takes an unexpected turn, there's only ever one question to ask: what's next?

I decided to take my focus and energy away from something that I couldn't change, and shift it in the direction of all the things that I wanted to create. So I wholeheartedly threw myself into finishing the manuscript that had been percolating for so long, and to ramping up my creativity working with Alicia on our Two Girls and an Elephant art. In the process, I tried not to wonder if the book would find a publisher or if the art would find an audience. My job was to joyfully do the work and see what would happen next.

A few months later, I was close to finishing the book, and Alicia and I had completed a wonderful collection of original oil-on-canvas paintings. And, right on cue, the miracles started to happen.

An acquaintance from Switzerland took a keen interest in our art, and set up two exhibitions for us there. It was an incredible opportunity for us to introduce our work in Europe, and for Alicia to have her first experience abroad.

Then I got a Facebook message from Tony Park saying that the crew that had filmed Johann and me for *House Hunters International* had just wrapped filming with him and Nicola, chronicling the purchase their South African home in Sabi Sands, a game reserve a few hours drive south of Hoedspruit. It turned out that they were the other couple the show had been considering when they'd interviewed us! The producers had found both stories so compelling that they'd decided to film them both. It seemed as if fate was making sure our paths would cross again.

Now that we were back in touch, I took the opportunity to ask Tony if I could send him my first draft. He was under a lot of pressure with a looming deadline of his own, but he quickly skimmed it and came back to me with some suggestions. He also recommended an editor I might use.

I reworked the manuscript and contacted the editor right away. My long-time friend Sarah, who's a brilliant graphic designer, created the perfect cover for what would soon be my first book. It was thrilling to see the project coming to life.

Once the editing was finished, I decided to ask Tony for a really big favour — would he consider writing the foreword for my now completed book, *The Gift of an Elephant?* In his typically generous fashion, he said it would be a pleasure. He sent the foreword, and when I read it, it brought tears to my eyes. I figured that if the book was even half as good as the foreword, I'd be satisfied.

The first time I held a printed copy of *The Gift of an Elephant* in my hands, I took it as concrete proof that if you stop doubting yourself and follow your desires, life will present you with the right people, circumstances and events to make those desires reality. I truly understood that the only thing that had ever stood in my way was me.

My police clearances from Canada arrived in plenty of time, and I set about preparing my application to renew my Relative's Permit in May, while at the same time getting things in order for my Permanent Residence application to be filed in July. Another chest X-ray was required, with two copies of the results. I needed a South African police clearance too, so we went to the police station, where an officer pressed my inky fingers in the appropriate boxes on the form and sent it off to Pretoria for processing.

When I went to pay for the police check, I requested two originals — one for the Relative's Permit and one for my Permanent Residence application.

The officer behind the counter looked at me quizzically. "Why would you want to pay for two clearances?" she asked.

I tried to explain.

"Right," she said, "but you don't need two police clearances. You just need one, and a copy."

"What's the difference?" I asked.

"Ninety-six rands," she replied. "You can get a certified copy free."

It was hard to argue with that logic.

The next step was to make an appointment with the office that handled the applications. I was dismayed to discover that I should've called much earlier — the next available appointment was at the end of May, a few days after the expiry date of my current permit. I took the appointment and hoped for the best.

Things are always working out for me. I repeat this mantra often, especially when waiting in line in any office that has to do with South African Home Affairs. And, sure enough, things do work out — eventually. It took three separate trips to Nelspruit, and jumping through a few hoops, but ultimately the application for my second Relative's Permit was accepted, on the condition that I report to the Immigration Department and get a letter saying that I was allowed to stay in the country while it was

185

being processed, since the previous one had expired. And the immigration officer who helped me actually extended the date on the letter to be sure that I wouldn't have to go back to renew it before the Relative's Permit came in.

Then it was time to turn my attention to the main event: in just a little over a month's time, I'd submit the paperwork for the first prize of visas, my Permanent Residence permit. Johann and I planned our anniversary celebration around filing the paperwork and booked an appointment with the Nelspruit office for the morning of 8 July, our fifth anniversary.

We set off the day before and took a leisurely drive through the Kruger National Park. As soon as we entered the main gate at Orpen, we were greeted by a big herd of elephants — that had to be a good omen.

As we continued down the road towards Satara Camp, one of the main camps in the park where we usually stopped for lunch, we saw a herd of buffalo, then, a little farther along, a young male lion by the side of the road finishing off the remains of an impala kill. Three of the iconic big five spotted before noon! Yes, it was going to be a great day.

After lunch we worked our way south through the park towards the town of Hazyview where we'd booked to spend the night. En route we encountered another herd of elephants and a pod of hippos splashing playfully in one of the dams.

It had been a perfect day in the Kruger, and as we settled into our hotel room for the night, we toasted our five years of marriage, the wonderful life we were creating in South Africa, and the success we were sure to have the next day filing my big stack of paperwork.

The next morning we arrived at the Home Affairs office in plenty of time for me to be screened by security and take my place in the first open seat in the already long line of people waiting. The room was crowded, so they asked that only the applicants wait in the office. Johann decided to wander around the adjacent mall to pass the time.

I pulled out the list of requirements for the visa one last time, and made sure that every piece of the documentation necessary was there and in order. When my name was called, I approached the counter with confidence.

The young woman behind the counter was friendly and familiar. We'd already met several times while I was filing for the Relative's Permit. She looked through all the paperwork, checking off each item as she made her way down the list. She paused, taking a long look at my South African police clearance.

When she looked up, I could see there was a problem and my gut told me it was going to be a big one. "This is a copy of the police clearance," she said. "Where's the original?"

I tried to stay calm. Surely this wasn't going to be an issue. Or was it...? "You have it. I mean, this office does. I gave it to you when I filed for my Relative's Permit last month."

"Oh, that's not good," she said. "You could have given me the certified copy for that. But for a Permanent Residence application, I have to have the original."

I struggled to swallow the feeling of panic that was quickly rising from my gut. Surely there had to be an easy solution to this!

"Could you get the original out of the other file, and swap it for the certified copy?" I ventured.

"No. I can't tamper with a file once it's in process. And even if I could, it's not here. It's gone to the Pretoria office."

I took a deep breath to calm down, but the tears were welling up in my eyes. "Okay. What can I do now?"

"Apply for another police clearance," she said.

"But that takes six weeks! I only have four weeks until my Canadian police clearance expires, then it will take at least six months to apply for another one from here! By then, the South African clearance will have expired, and I'll have to apply for that all over again!" I felt the noose of red tape tightening around my throat as I tried to explain the bureaucratic nightmare that was about to be unleashed on me, all because I'd unknowingly handed in the wrong piece of paper.

"Sometimes they come in faster," she said, trying to reassure me. "Go to the police station now and hope for a miracle."

She'd said exactly the right word. That was what I had to do — except I had to *expect* the miracle, not just hope for it.

I left the office to find Johann. I quickly explained what had happened, and we went to the Nelspruit police station, where I once again completed the inky-finger exercise. I paid the fee, asking if there was any way to speed up the process. Apparently there wasn't.

I tried to view this as a perfect opportunity to practise my new beliefs. Whenever I thought about the police clearance, I'd visualize getting the message that it had been processed and was ready for collection. I'd picture myself leaving the police station with the document in my hand, and walking over to the immigration office, where they'd accept my application for permanent residence.

Over the next four weeks, any time I caught myself worrying about it, I'd stop and take a deep breath, close my eyes and repeat the visualization. Then I'd turn my attention to other things, until the thought came up again, and I'd repeat the process.

The weeks passed slowly, and no word came about the police clearance. I decided to call the main police station in Pretoria to see where my fingerprints were in what was surely a large pile of prints waiting to be processed. I called and called, but no one answered the phone.

I decided to try email, and surprisingly got a response almost right away. The clearance was in process and should be done in four or five days. I wrote back immediately, thanking the officer profusely for her reply, and asking if it could possibly be done in four days — five days would be too late, as my Canadian police clearance would have expired.

Another response came the following day. Yes, it would likely be done but there was no guarantee. They would send me a message with an authorization number that would allow me to pick it up as soon as it had been processed.

The night before my Canadian police clearance was about to expire, I still hadn't received the message and I was struggling not to lose my faith in the miracle. Once again, I closed my eyes and pictured myself walking out of the police station with the document, and walking into the immigration office, where they accepted the application.

Then I had a sudden, alarming thought. "What if the clearance comes in late in the morning and they don't get around to sending the message to us until the afternoon? We won't have time to drive down there and get to the immigration office to submit the application," I said to Johann. "If we're sitting here in Hoedspruit and we get a message that it's in Nelspruit tomorrow afternoon, I'll never forgive myself. I know it's a two-hour drive and could be a complete waste of petrol, but I think we should drive to Nelspruit and go to the police station tomorrow morning to see if the clearance is there."

"Okay," Johann replied tentatively, "but without the authorization number, will you be able to pick it up even if it is there?"

"We'll cross that bridge when we come to it," I said, hoping that the bridge would in fact be there to cross.

We arrived at the police station the next morning, and made our way up the three flights of stairs to the office where the clearances were handed out. There was no one behind the desk, and after we'd spent a few minutes anxiously pacing up and down the hallway, an officer who'd been watching us took pity on us and went to find the man we needed to see.

Once he'd settled in behind his desk, I asked if the latest batch of clearances had arrived.

"Yes," he said, "about an hour ago. I'm just going to send off the notices now."

"Oh, sir," I said, barely able to breathe, "could you please check to see if mine is there?"

191

He asked my name, then licked his thumb and started paging through the pile.

Anxiously watching from the other side of the desk, I was sure I spotted my name.

"Please, go back one!" I exclaimed. Sure enough, it had my name on it. "That's mine!"

"Oh, good," he said, and handed it to me, no questions asked.

As we hurried down the stairs I started giggling almost uncontrollably. "Can you believe it?" I said to Johann. "It was there, and he just handed it to me — without an authorization number or even asking to see my passport!"

"Keep running," my husband replied, "before he realizes that and takes it back!"

There was no time to waste. We raced out of the dark building and into the bright sunlight. It felt like my feet weren't even touching the pavement as we hurried the three blocks to the office where I'd finally submit my Permanent Residence application.

We entered the building and took the lift up to the all-too-familiar office. I was very surprised to see that there was no queue of people waiting to get in, and a quick look through the glass door of the waiting room revealed that no one was waiting inside. Was it closed? Was this some kind of holiday we didn't know about? Elation was quickly turning to dismay.

A young man came to the door.

"Are you closed?" I asked.

"No," he said. "Come on in."

As per usual, he checked my passport and quickly scanned me with the metal-detector wand.

I walked through the door, but he stopped Johann. "I need to see your ID book," he said.

It hadn't occurred to Johann to bring his identification document on this trip and he said, "No problem, I'll just wait here while you go in to file the papers." It felt so strange walking into that familiar place, without the usual crowd waiting in line. I'd never seen it empty before. That was another miracle in itself!

I approached the woman at the counter, who recognized me immediately. She smiled. "It came in?"

"Yes, the miracle happened!" I exclaimed.

She set about her usual routine, paging through the required documents and ticking them off on the master list as she went. She got to the Canadian police clearance. "This expires today," she observed.

"Yes — which is why it's a good thing the other one came in today," I said.

She continued with her work, and, after having checked the pile thoroughly twice, she asked, "Where's your letter of support?"

"What's that?" I asked as I felt the blood start to drain from my face.

"The letter of support from your husband to say he'll look after you until you're legally allowed to work and able to find a job."

"I can get one right now," I said, greatly relieved. "He's just outside the door. He's forgotten his ID, so the security guard won't let him come in, but can I take him a paper and pen so he can write the letter?"

After a quick consultation with the security guard, it was decided that Johann could in fact come in and write the letter. He just wasn't sure what to write.

"If I were you," advised the young woman kindly, "I'd say that you'll support your wife financially and emotionally while you await the outcome of the application."

Johann dutifully wrote down what were obviously key words that would ensure the acceptance of the letter. He signed it and handed it to her. She inserted it in the appropriate place in the pile of paperwork.

With the file now complete, she placed the pages in the centre of a manila folder with two flaps. She methodically closed the left flap, then the right. Then placed the folder in a navy-blue cloth bag and zipped it shut. She handed it to me and motioned for me to move to my left, to the next window along.

I took a step to the left, then handed the cloth bag to the man behind the counter. He unzipped it and took out the folder. He opened the right flap, then the left, and started to look through the pile, now adding his check marks beside the marks the young woman had made as she'd gone through the requirement list.

Eventually he got to the Canadian police clearance. "This expires today," he observed.

"Yes, it does," I said. I glanced at Johann, who avoided my eyes. It was getting to be quite comical, but it would be no laughing matter if one of the officials decided that the application wasn't acceptable.

After what seemed like an eternity, he finished his inspection of the paperwork and placed it back in the folder, closing the flaps and sliding it back into the cloth bag, before zipping it closed and handing it back to me.

"How would you like to pay?"

I quickly found the credit card in my wallet and eagerly handed it over.

"What's this?" he asked.

"It's a Mastercard from my bank in Canada."

"Sorry, we don't take foreign cards."

Johann reached into his wallet and pulled out his bank card. The clerk tried twice to run it through the machine. Both times it was rejected.

"Must be a problem with the machine," the man said.

Johann said he'd run to the bank and get cash, but the man decided to try once more. The third time was a charm, and the application was paid for. With only twenty minutes to go before the office closed for the day, we were almost in the clear. But there was still one more hurdle to jump.

"Have a seat here," the man said, indicating one of two chairs outside a small office with a closed door, on which he knocked. "She'll be with you now." "She" was the supervisor.

His use of the word "now" was encouraging, but as I looked up at the clock and saw that the office would be closing in half an hour, I became concerned. In South Africa, time is generally expressed in three ways: "now", "just now" and "now-now". When I first arrived in the country, I assumed that "now" meant immediately. I then reasoned that "just now" would mean in a few minutes, and that "now-now", with its repeated use of the imperative, must mean that it was doubly urgent. Boy, did I have that all wrong!

In my experience, "now" means soon or soon-ish; it's never clearly defined. "Just now" means you could be waiting a few hours. And the dreaded "now-now" means sometime between later and whenever, and quite possibly never. Because he'd said "now", there was at least hope that the supervisor would see me before the clock struck four and the office closed for the day.

And luck remained with me, because within just a few minutes a woman opened the door and called me in. She took the cloth bag from me and placed it on her desk. She unzipped the bag, pulled out the file, and opened the right flap, then the left. She checked all the documents, stopping at the Canadian police clearance to observe that it expired that day. At that point I didn't know whether to laugh or cry.

Once satisfied that all my paperwork was in order, it was time for her to ask me a few questions and take my fingerprints. The questions were easy, but the fingerprints turned out to be another ordeal. No black ink here: this office was high tech. But for some reason, the sensor pad had a hard time picking up my prints. She tried over and over again, rolling my fingers across the screen, but each time the print was rejected. She pressed my fingers down harder. I looked up at the clock and began panicking, realizing that the office would be closing in just a few minutes.

We both took a step back from the machine.

"Okay," she said, "let me clean the screen, and you wipe off your hands with this sanitizer."

She sprayed a solvent on the screen and wiped it down while I removed any traces of oil sweat from my fingertips.

"Now, let's try this again."

This time, like magic, all ten prints went into the system. The application had been accepted just before the close of the business day.

"You made it!" she exclaimed. "You can expect to be a permanent resident of South Africa in eight to ten months' time.

High-school graduate Butrus

Paulus meets his match

Author Tony Park and me at Tanda Tula

Chapter 10

Time flies when you're having fun, so I made it a point to focus on just that — doing the things that made me happy.

Tracy and I started doing morning walks in the wilderness area of Zandspruit Bush and Aero Estate. Of the thousand or so hectares of property that made up the estate, 600 had been left undeveloped so the animals could roam freely. We'd set out bright and early, any time between 5 and 5:30am. We had to go that early — it was summer, and if we left any later it was just too hot, with temperatures often hitting 30 degrees Celsius by 7am. After all my years of 3:30am wake-ups when I was on the radio, I bristled at the thought of getting up before 5, but the prospect of walking among the zebras and wildebeest was enough to get me out of bed. Besides, it was already light before 5, and the birds' dawn chorus was well underway, calling me out from under the covers.

Our morning ritual took about an hour and a half, and covered about seven kilometres from the front gate, through the estate to the wilderness area, where we did a big loop and came back again. It wasn't long before the animals got used to our presence and we were able to approach closer and closer without causing any alarm. Watching the sun rise while standing just a few metres from a tower of giraffes is an absolutely extraordinary experience.

The wonderful thing about the bush is that it's not predictable; each day is a new adventure. You never know what will cross your path.

I'd just parked my car at the entrance to the property and walked through the gate on my way to meet Tracy when I had the overwhelming feeling that there were eyes on me. I stopped in my tracks, carefully scanning the tall grass. Something was coming towards me, but I had no idea what.

Suddenly, an African wild dog appeared on the path just a few metres in front of me. He stopped, and we looked at each other, each deciding if the other was a threat. I cast down my eyes so he wouldn't think I was being aggressive or challenging him. I'd read in *Africa Geographic* that there'd never been a recorded incident of an African wild dog in the wild attacking a human, but it still seemed like a good idea to act submissively.

After a few seconds he obviously decided I wasn't a threat, nor was I of any particular interest, and he turned and trotted away. It was thrilling to have such a close encounter with such a rare and beautiful creature — and on foot, no less!

And it wasn't over. Another dog emerged from the grass, stopping in the exact same spot, giving me the once-over and continuing on behind the first. Then a third dog appeared, followed by a fourth. Each stopped to look at me, then nonchalantly carried on.

As I watched them trot away, I was startled by the ping of the cellphone in my pocket. I pulled it out and saw a message from Tracy: "Heads up — wild dogs on the property." I burst out laughing. I'd decided that I'd enjoy each and every day, and every day I found more to enjoy.

Johann and I spent many happy afternoons cruising around Khaya Ndlovu before finding a beautiful spot in the dry riverbed to enjoy the sunset. We'd found a particular spot that was a popular crossing for animals. We'd plant our chairs in the loose sand, then settle in to see what would appear. The usual suspects were the baboons and the mischievous vervet monkeys, who would lounge around, and play with and groom each other. There were also plenty of antelopes: impala, nyala, kudu and sometimes herds of wildebeest.

In this location, even the ordinary seemed magical, and when the extraordinary occurred, it was absolutely incredible.

On a couple of occasions we saw herds of elephants crossing. They never even noticed us. But we certainly were of interest to a group of giraffes that crossed the sand, flanking us on both sides. We counted sixteen, a few babies among them. Some were walking, but others ran, kicking up sand as they passed. Their gait is so graceful that even those who were running appeared to be moving in slow motion.

Once they'd finished their crossing, they doubled back to take a better look at us. Most of them stood a fair distance away, but three of them kept advancing, stopping every few metres before deciding to move a little closer. I actually started to get a bit nervous. While generally quite docile, a giraffe can kill a lion with one kick, and when the males fight for dominance, bashing their long, strong necks together, it can be to the death. But we were no threat to them, I reminded myself, and we sat calmly and waited to see what would happen.

They moved closer and closer until they were standing up on the riverbank, right in front of us. We all looked at each other for a long time. The bush went very quiet.

Then we heard a faint sound, almost like a soft meow. Johann and I looked at each other, questioning if that was in fact what we'd heard. It was the first time either of us had ever heard a giraffe vocalize, and it certainly wasn't a sound we'd expected!

After about half an hour, just as it was starting to get dark, the giraffes, their curiosity satisfied, ambled away.

Also high up on the list of thrilling riverbed experiences was an encounter with the cheetah boys — two brothers well known in our area. We'd invited our friends Kerry and Eric along and we were enjoying our sundown drinks when Eric spotted something. It turned out to be two somethings, with spots! The cheetah boys were accustomed to humans but by no stretch of the imagination could they be considered tame.

As they walked towards us, Kerry asked if we should run for the Land Rover.

"That's the worst thing we could do," I assured her. "Running makes you something to chase. Let's look as big as we can, and just keep talking. If we don't react, maybe they won't either."

I must've taken a hundred pictures as the boys came astonishingly close and flopped down on some rocks that were still radiating heat from the afternoon sun. They hung around for a few minutes, then stood up and stretched. They walked past the Land Rover and back into the bush. Just another day in Africa!

Here, even the simplest of things can be an adventure — like using the outdoor shower. One morning, as I shampooed my hair, I looked around and realized I had company. A gorgeous little sunbird with an iridescent-green head was busy building a nest for his female in a plant just an arm's length away from me; an agama, a lizard with a striking blue head, sat on top of the shower wall; and Paulus peacock was perched on the poles that provided a privacy fence.

Life had turned out to be good for our peacock friend. I don't know what he'd done to finally win her over — or maybe he just wore her down over time — but eventually Penelope relented and accepted Paulus as her mate. There was no fanfare. One day, she just hopped up and joined him on the railing of our back patio, his preferred perch. They sat together but not like love birds. They were more like bookends: he on one end, she on the other. If it would never be a great romance, at least they appeared content.

As for Johann and I, what we felt for each other far exceeded contentment. The absolute luxury of being together all the time had made our bond even stronger. Rarely did a day go by without one of us saying to the other what had become our mantra: "I choose you again today." And soon we had a beautiful opportunity to prove it.

We were attending a charity auction with Alicia and Rob when an item came up for bids that was just too perfect to pass up. It was a weekend at Garonga Safari Camp, a gorgeous place about an hour outside of town. Coincidentally, it was the place where Johann and I had gotten married when we'd eloped nearly five years before.

We'd so often reminisced about our perfect wedding, and we knew that it was exactly the type of ceremony our friends had dreamed of too. While Alicia and Rob had been together for years, they'd never actually tied the knot, and it was something they both really wanted to do.

I was fast off the mark with the bidding, and when the gavel came down, we suddenly had a wedding and a vows renewal to plan!

I thought it couldn't have been more perfect — and then it was. My dear friend Denise, who'd been with me in South Sudan when Johann and I met, let us know she was coming to visit. She'd already booked her flight, completely unaware that we were planning a second wedding. We were thrilled to realize that the dates lined up and she'd be there with us. We'd receive the ultimate gift: Denise singing our wedding song.

The day dawned sunny and warm — a perfect winter's day in South Africa. As we drove out to Garonga for the ceremonies, there was all of the excitement of our elopement and none of the nerves.

It had been five years since we'd stood on that platform in the trees overlooking the waterhole. At that time, we hardly knew each other but we'd taken a complete leap of faith and had promised to make a life together. We'd had no idea of how we'd make it work. The intervening years had done little to give us clarity on the "how" but the time had made us even more certain that we'd find a way.

The wedding was to take place first, and the intimate party assembled on the platform: Rob and Alicia, their children James and Amy, and Alicia's mother Eleina. Johann and I took up our positions as the best man and matron of honour. Denise's soulful voice soared as she serenaded the happy couple with the classic Stevie Wonder love song "You and I".

The bride was stunning with her long dark hair flowing over her shoulders. Her strapless dress was vibrant blue, a shade that matched the topaz earrings I'd worn on my wedding day. They had been my "something blue" but today, for Alicia, they took on the role of "something borrowed". Rob looked smart in a pressed black shirt and jeans — about as formal as it gets for guys in the bush.

Their wedding ceremony echoed Johann's and mine, a mix of Christian and tribal traditions, including the gift of a blanket to the bride symbolizing her groom's commitment to keep her protected and warm. She presented him with a gourd symbolizing her commitment to comfort and nourish him. It was a beautiful, emotional ceremony, exactly the wedding they'd hoped for.

After all the hugs, kisses and congratulations, it was Johann's and my turn to renew our vows. I kept thinking how absolutely miraculous it was to have returned to the place where we'd run off on our own, but now we were renewing our vows surrounded by friends who were like family and this incredible place had become our home.

Denise sang "our" song, "History in the Making" by Darius Rucker. As she sang the lyrics that are inscribed in our wedding rings — "last first kiss" in Johann's and "a chance worth taking" in mine — I became completely overwhelmed and couldn't hold back the tears. I was completely in love, with my husband and with my life.

Wanting to make the most of our time with Denise, we invited some friends over for a party and jam session on the back patio. Denise's beautiful voice was being accompanied by the guitar stylings of our friend Joel.

We noticed, moving among our guests, a furry party crasher with beautiful green eyes. The cat obviously had good taste in music.

She made her rounds, rubbing up against legs and occasionally jumping up on someone's lap. When the music stopped, she disappeared into the darkness.

The next night, we were eating dinner on the patio, and the cat came back. After receiving sufficient affection from Johann and me, and even from Denise, who insists she doesn't like cats, the animal disappeared again.

By the next night, the cat was sitting on Denise's lap, and by the time my friend was leaving to return to Canada, even she had to admit that there was something very special about this little creature.

The cat was remarkably silent. In fact, at first we wondered if she even could meow. But the most unusual thing about her was that I, who am terribly allergic to cats, seemed to be fine with her.

Soon, she was sleeping in the house, but as a precaution we closed the bedroom door and she slept on the sofa in the lounge. After a few nights, I still wasn't having an adverse reaction to her, so we opened the bedroom door, allowing her to join us if she chose. Of course, from that point on, she completely took over our hearts and much more than her fair share of our bed.

We'd been adopted by a cat. Now that she was part of the family, we had to give her a name. We settled on Ntumbela in honour of one of my favourite leopards from my days at Tanda Tula. We called her Bella for short.

Bella seemed to get on well with the other creatures at the lodge — she fit right in. She'd sit out on the back deck sunning herself, idly watching the little birds flitting from tree branch to birdbath and then down to the ground to eat the seed we'd scattered. The larger francolins and guineafowl didn't bother her; in fact, she found the guineafowl of particular interest and seemed to actually want to communicate with them.

We had a group of sixteen who were regular customers at our "bird café". We threw down seed for them early in the morning and again late in the afternoon. One of the first sounds we ever heard Bella make was in response to the loud cackling of the blue-headed birds who were pecking away at their sundown snack. She watched and listened for a while, then, looking directly at them, she opened her mouth and emitted a noise that sounded a bit like gargling. She still "speaks" to them regularly and they do seem to answer, but we have no idea if any of them understand what's being said.

Even Paulus, whom we expected to be quite intimidating to Bella, given his large stature and piercing cry, didn't faze her. She wasn't bothered when he hopped up on the patio and walked past her. He often helped himself to her cat-food pellets and she didn't seem to mind that either, rarely even interrupting her nap to pay him any attention at all.

Penelope, on the other hand, was a completely different matter. In the peahen, Bella had met her nemesis.

As soon as the cat caught sight of that bird, she would jump up and bolt into the house. This turned out to be a serious tactical error on Bella's part: Penelope knew that she had the upper hand in their territorial dispute and she became downright aggressive.

Before long, she wasn't content with just having the enemy retreat; the bird wanted to provoke a fight. She'd pace up and down the length of the house, looking through the sliding glass doors to try to spot the cat inside. Bella often hid, but sometimes she'd get feisty and show herself. From her secure position on the other side of the glass, Bella would assume a crouched "attack" position and hiss vehemently at the big bully. These stand-offs wouldn't end until Johann or I chased Penny away.

Eventually, we had to ban Penelope from the patio completely, and the two settled into an uneasy truce.

Our furry friend was an absolute delight to have around, always docile and affectionate. As humans are prone to do, we thought of her as "our" cat. I worried when she went out after dark, fearing that she would have a run-in with one of the large porcupines with very sharp quills that roamed the property at night, or, even worse, with one of the fierce honey badgers we knew were around. Those small but mighty creatures will take on anything, including lions. If Bella were to get in the path of a honey badger, she wouldn't stand a chance.

It was always a huge relief to me when I saw her standing at the patio door, waiting to be let in, when she'd finished her wandering and was ready to settle in for the night.

One evening, I let her in and gave her dinner as usual. A short time later, she was back at the patio door, wanting to be let out again. It was already dark, so I decided against it. I picked her up and put her on my lap, hoping the affection would distract her. She indulged me for a few minutes, but then jumped down and went back to the patio door, looking up at me expectantly. I really wanted her to stay in, so I looked away, ignoring her request. A few minutes later, she jumped up next to me on the couch, and when she had my full attention, she looked me straight in the eye and peed on the cushion.

I was completely shocked. It was so out of character! My reaction was to give her a swat on the bum, which sent her to hide behind the couch. I regretted my impulse immediately, and tried to talk her into emerging from her hiding place but she stubbornly refused.

When Johann got home, she was still in hiding, and I explained what had happened.

"Are you sure she did it on purpose?" he asked. "Maybe she just had an accident."

"I really don't think so," I replied. "It seemed so deliberate, the way she made sure she had my attention before she did it. But you know what's weird? There was no hostility or defiance in her eyes; I think she was just telling me in no uncertain terms that she isn't interested in following my rules."

"I think you may be reading too much into this," he reasoned.

My gut told me I wasn't, but it made me feel better to consider that possibility. Perhaps it was all in my imagination.

The next night, Bella made sure the message was crystal clear. She came in from her walkabout just as it was getting dark, and ate dinner as usual. Shortly after, once again she stood by the door, waiting to be let out. Johann and I ignored her and sat down to watch TV.

After a few minutes, Bella jumped up on his lap, gave him that same even gaze, and peed right on him!

What could we do? It was already obvious who was going to win this clash of wills. It suddenly became very clear to me that she *wasn't* "our" cat. She lived with us because she chose to, not because she belonged to us.

"Cat wants her freedom," I concluded.

"Yes, she does. But are you going to be able to sleep at night?" Johann asked. "You always worry so much when she's out after dark."

"I've decided to stop worrying. She managed just fine before she found us. She's smart. I have to trust her to know what's best for her."

There was much to be learned from observing a cat. I'd been learning from Bella since the day she moved in, seeing her as the ultimate Zen master. She didn't have to do anything except be herself. She did exactly as she pleased, with no thought to my expectations, and as a result, she was always content and relaxed. It truly was a pleasure being around her.

Her peaceful presence always brought me joy. It wasn't until I'd misguidedly tried to control her that we'd developed a problem. I'd made a huge mistake when I'd assumed that because I loved her, I knew what was best for her.

Her reaction was a reminder of that important lesson I was obviously still trying to learn: my love for someone, human or animal, doesn't make me in charge of them or responsible for their wellbeing. My job in this life is simple — it's to mind my own business.

That phrase has taken on quite a negative connotation, but if you take it at face value, there's no better advice for living. Focus on your life and tend to it the way you see fit, while giving others the freedom to do the same. Observe but don't judge. Cat wants her freedom. Don't we all?

Each of us has a life to live, and I think our real responsibility in this world is to take charge of that life, rejoice in it at every opportunity, and make it thrive. When you do that, there's no limit to what you can offer others.

I believe that by choosing to be happy, I can enable my presence to be of benefit to those around me. Joy and happiness are contagious and lead to so many other wonderful things, like enthusiasm, creativity, generosity and love. You can't give what you don't have, so strive to fill yourself with peace, love and joy, and there'll be plenty to share. I believe this is how we change the world.

I'd spent months focusing on the things that made me happy: being with my husband and the true friends I'd made, revelling in our beautiful environment, and observing and interacting with all the wonderful creatures living with and around us. I was enjoying writing and creating art. The only thing missing was the opportunity to teach. And, of course, when I was ready, that opportunity appeared too.

Our doctor friend Wendy had left her job running the surgical ward at Tintswalo Hospital in the village of Acornhoek, one of South Africa's seemingly forgotten communities. Poverty and HIV are rampant in the area, with unemployment estimated at sixty percent and a staggering one in three people HIV positive. Many homes are shacks that don't have electricity, and even the brick homes don't have running water.

Wendy's five years as a doctor in that community had given her a deep empathy for the people and valuable insights into the problems they faced. She took over as the director of Seeds of Light, an NGO (non-governmental organization) dedicated to supporting and uplifting impoverished and marginalized communities through practical projects. When Wendy put out a call for help for one of their projects, the Ekurhuleni Centre for Orphans and Vulnerable Children, my friend Nicola and I both put up our hands.

Ekurhuleni means "place of peace", but with over a hundred children flocking to the centre each day, it was a vibrant, noisy hive of activity. It truly was a refuge for these children, a place where people cared for them. It was also a place with running water and electricity, where they were fed what would often be their only meal of the day.

Wendy had hoped we could help some of the older children pass their exams; I would tutor English and Nicola would take on the maths. But that idea proved difficult to execute. The children were always so excited when we arrived, and they all wanted to be part of whatever we were doing, so we were never able just to work with the older children. Given the sheer number of children, ranging in age from toddlers to teenagers, we had to approach it from a different angle. As South Africans are so fond of saying, we had to "make a plan". In a country where things seldom unfold as expected, that expression is pretty much the national mantra.

We tried to carry on with lessons, dividing up the group, and teaching maths in the main building and English in the centre's library, but there were still too many students at too many different age levels for one teacher to manage. After a few weeks, we decided it was better to join forces and do an activity that everyone would enjoy. Remembering how much my friends at Tanda Tula had enjoyed fables — traditional stories that explained things like how the lion became king of the animals and why the warthog eats on bended knee — we decided to tell stories. Each week we'd choose a story, then rewrite it in simple English.

Despite that effort, many of the children still couldn't understand. Luckily, we had a couple of star pupils whose English was excellent, so they would help out. Lovely Linkje and the very aptly named Brilliant would translate the stories into Shangaan, and we'd act out the scenes, trying to teach English words as we did. While this programme didn't fulfil the original goal, it did at least expose the children to more English — and it was fun.

It also became apparent that we were accomplishing something else equally important: were building familiarity and trust.

For so many of the children, white people were a complete curiosity. Despite the fact that Hoedspruit, which has a predominantly white population, is geographically nearby, it's a world apart. Most of these children had never been out of their villages, and for them, white faces were extremely rare.

The fact that we showed up each week let them know that other people — even white people — cared about them.

Initially, some of the children shied away from us, unsure if it was safe to approach. But the vast majority accepted us with open arms — literally. We'd be greeted with hugs and many children wanting to hold our hands as we made our way down to the library. Luckily, there were also several volunteers who wanted to carry our books, bags and water bottles, which freed us up to have as many children as possible grabbing on to each of our fingers, our arms and legs.

After a rousing session in which we learned how the ostrich got its long neck, we were making our way back to the car for the hour-long drive home. Linkje was walking alongside me, carrying my schoolbag. As usual, several other children were walking with me, holding on to my hands. A very young boy walked over to her and said something to her in Shangaan.

Her eyes opened wide in surprise and she stopped in her tracks. "Do you know what he just said?" she exclaimed.

"No, I didn't understand. What did he say?"

"He said that they shouldn't hold your hand because you are white!"

I was caught completely off guard, but tried not to act surprised and to take it in stride. "Oh. Please tell him that of course they can hold my hand. It's absolutely fine — we're friends. Friends hold hands."

Linkje dutifully translated my words for the boy but he didn't look convinced and gave a retort that once again rattled my young friend.

"Do you know what he said now?" she cried out, clearly dismayed.

"No, please tell me."

"He said the reason they shouldn't hold your hand is because you will turn black!"

That was a new one on me. I considered my reply and tried to word it carefully. "Well, you can tell him that I don't think that's true. I've held hands with lots of people, and I've never seen anyone change colour. And even if it were true and I did turn black, that would be okay."

Linkje turned to him and translated my explanation.

The young boy shook his head and walked away.

I wondered which part of my statement had been the most difficult for him to believe.

Close encounters: African wild dog and cheetah

Denise and the happy couples at the wedding/vow-renewal ceremony

Bella

A lesson with Linkje

Chapter 11

You know that feeling, when things start falling into place and everything is going well? For some people, it invokes apprehension. They think that because things are going so well, something is inevitably about to go terribly wrong.

Others roll with the feeling, and in fact often refer to it as being "on a roll".

What I've come to believe is that we're the ones who create that momentum, one way or the other. How we choose to interpret any situation influences what happens next. I think we keep things moving in our desired direction by focusing on the things that make us happy, and by expecting good things to happen. And from my own experience I can say that the better it gets, the better it gets. For me, 2015 had been a year of living purposefully, testing this theory and watching the results — and I was definitely on a roll!

As the year drew to a close, October saw me on my way back to Canada, excitedly anticipating the launch of *The Gift of an Elephant.* I'd be speaking at a women's conference called "The Power of the Purse", an event that had been created by my very dynamic friend Cynthia. In my former life as a radio personality, she'd asked me to be the master of ceremonies at the inaugural event. I never would've guessed that seven years later I'd be returning to the conference as one of the speakers, with a marvellous story to share.

The day after my talk would be the official launch of my book at *Music, Art and Africa* — a Two Girls and an Elephant art show, as well as a performance by Denise. The proceeds from that evening would support the art-and-music camp in South Sudan where Johann and I had met. It thrilled me to see all of my passions coming together in one amazing event.

When I arrived in Canada, I went straight home to Penetanguishene to see my parents, grateful for the opportunity to spend time with them. A few days later, Lynn arrived, bringing with her the very first printed copies of my book. We tore open the box and she put a copy in my mother's hands. Mom absolutely beamed with pride.

After a week of reconnecting with family and friends, I made my way down to London. The night before the conference, I had dinner with Cynthia. I confided in her how nervous I was about speaking the next day. That's when she informed me that due to a scheduling conflict, the keynote speaker for the event would have to leave early. She'd moved me into the keynote position.

I was terrified! It had been six years since I'd left the world of media and public appearances, and I'd spent several of those years in near isolation when Johann was away working. This was going to be one hell of a reintroduction to public life, with three hundred women expected to attend.

I was actually glad I'd only found out about my "promotion" to keynote speaker the night before, because really there was nothing more that I could do. It was too late to make any changes; I'd just have to deliver the talk I'd prepared and hope for the best.

"Things are always working out for me." I repeated my belief over and over again as I paced in my hotel room that night, and practised my speech one last time.

The next morning was a bit of a blur. Denise picked me up and we arrived at the conference. I saw many friendly and familiar faces in the crowd. I was still really nervous but I tried to focus on why I wanted to share my story. I'd always had a truly good life, but my experiences in Africa had given me a whole new perspective on life and I was a much happier person than I'd ever been before. If anything I'd learned might resonate with someone in that room and in some way encourage her to take a step towards the life she'd always imagined, then that was reason enough for me to face my fear and share some of my experiences.

I paced nervously backstage while I was being introduced. I don't remember climbing the stairs to the stage, but suddenly I found myself in the spotlight. I'd worked hard to memorize what I wanted to say, but at the last minute I decided to bring my script onstage with me, for fear that my mind would go completely blank in front of an audience.

Of course, if I'd actually wanted to be able to read that script, I would have to swallow my vanity and put on my glasses.

As I looked out into the sea of expectant faces, I figured the best way to start was by being honest. I held up my script and my glasses and said, "I can't decide what I miss more, my eyesight or my mind." That drew a laugh and I relaxed a bit and began to tell my story.

When I'd finished, I walked off the stage and into the open arms of an old friend from my radio days who was doing the sound for the event. Don gave me a big hug, then physically turned me around to look back out at the audience. "Look," he said. "They're giving you a standing ovation."

There was a long line at the book-signing table after my speech, and I sold lots of books, but more importantly, four of the women in that queue made virtually the same comment: "You came here to speak to me today." My truth had resonated with them, and just might play a small part in helping them to make changes in their lives. That possibility made me truly happy.

The next night, *Music, Art and Africa* was a pure celebration. Lynn had done an incredible job of organizing the event at London's premier venue, the Grand Theatre. Family, friends and former colleagues all attended. It was there that the amazing reality really hit me.

As a child, I'd been fascinated by Africa. I'd wanted to be a writer and an artist when I grew up. And now, my life was made up of all those things! I'd found not only the love of my life in Africa, but I'd rediscovered my authentic self. I'd also created the life I'd always wanted to live.

After spending a particularly thankful Thanksgiving with my family, I returned to South Africa, but for less than a month.

On 17 November, Alicia and I had a plane to catch.

We were soaring, both figuratively and literally. Midnight found us on an Air France plane, toasting the arrival of Alicia's birthday with French champagne in plastic cups. We were on our way to Switzerland for two Two Girls and an Elephant art shows!

The acquaintance who'd approached us about introducing our art to Europe had now become a good friend. Ron had arranged for our paintings to be displayed at Macelleria D'Arte, a gallery in the charming Swiss town of St Gallen, then a week later the collection would move to a wine event being held in the same area. We were very excited at the prospect of having our work featured alongside some fine South African wines.

Ron and his South African fiancée Adel were the perfect hosts and tour guides, showing us around St Gallen.

We stayed as guests of the management at Schloss Wartensee, a historic castle that had been turned into a luxurious boutique hotel. We sat in our room, celebrating, this time with French champagne in crystal glasses, as we watched snowflakes float gently past our window. It was like being in a fairytale — and all this, just two years after starting our artistic collaboration together. It was absolutely incredible!

In between the two art events, Alicia and I decided to take full advantage of being in Europe. We took the opportunity to make a quick trip to France to explore Paris with all its glorious art and architecture. It was Alicia's first time travelling outside South Africa, and she'd always wanted to see Paris. I'd visited the City of Lights when I was 18 years old, and only for a day, when I took one of those manic thirteen-countries-in-fourteen days tours. Exploring the city at our leisure and on foot would be a completely different experience. We were both giddy with excitement.

We took the TGV — *train à grande vitesse* — the high-speed train from Zurich to Paris. Travelling at three hundred kilometres an hour, the time and the scenery flew by. In a little over four hours we arrived at the Gare de Lyon.

From there, we took the metro to the third arrondissement, then walked the few blocks to the studio apartment we'd rented for four glorious days. It was on the top floor of a four-storey walk-up, but even lugging our bags up the steep staircase didn't dampen our enthusiasm.

We set out immediately on foot, meandering along the Seine to the Champs-Élysées to experience the delights of the famous Paris Christmas Market. Darkness fell as we made our way to the famous boulevard. Christmas lights sparkled and the scent of spicy mulled wine and roasted chestnuts filled the air. It was cold, with a dusting of snow on the ground, and a few flakes in the air. Our first stop was at a booth selling wool hats and gloves. We each purchased an authentic French beret to help keep us warm.

For me, it felt like Christmas should. For Alicia, who'd grown up in a place where the holiday is celebrated around the pool in the oppressive heat of the South African summer, it was absolutely magical to experience Christmas as she'd only seen it in movies and on TV.

We spent the next few days walking all over the city and taking in all the sights — Notre Dame, Montmartre and, of course, the Eiffel Tower. And the museums with their incredible collections of famous works by Monet, Manet, Degas and Picasso. It was hard to believe that we were actually seeing such famous works of art in person!

While we were soaking up all Paris had to offer, a bit of drama was unfolding at home. A message from Johann revealed that Penelope peahen was missing. She hadn't been seen for several days, and Paulus peacock was wandering around like a lost soul. We worried that a honey badger or some other animal might have gotten her. She'd always been too feisty for her own good. We once saw a jackal running on the property, and were stunned to see Penelope chasing after him. He was never seen around those parts again.

As it turned out, there was no cause for alarm. The mystery of Penelope's disappearance was solved a few days later when she was found holed up in the outdoor shower of one of the rental units in the complex. She was sitting on eggs! The improbable couple had finally consummated their relationship and Paulus was about to become a father.

The chicks had hatched just before I got home from Switzerland but they hadn't made an appearance yet. Penelope kept them hidden for a few days, but soon after my homecoming, Johann and I spied her making her way through the tall grass in the back garden, clucking softly and herding her brood as she came towards our house. There were four tiny, fuzzy chicks, two of them yellow and two of them mostly brown with patterns on their backs and wings — two boys and two girls!

Then the father appeared — the proverbial proud peacock. Paulus was surrounded by his miracles.

And I was surrounded by all of mine.

Paulus, Penelope and family, and Johann and I, creating our "happily ever afters" every day

Epilogue

Raptors' Lodge, Hoedspruit, South Africa, April 2017. Time flies — and so do peacocks! It's already been a year since Paulus and Penelope produced their first brood, and now three new chicks have arrived, this time three boys.

The original group of four was taken to a nearby farm when they were 10 months old — too many noisy peacocks living on one small property does not make for happy residents. I do miss them, but I get to see them from time to time because they still remember their first home and sometimes fly in for a visit.

Penelope is already teaching her new brood to fly, taking them up on our back patio and encouraging them to jump off and flap their wings. If history is any indicator, it won't be long before she has them flying up on to our thatched roof and jumping from there.

This second round of motherhood seems to have mellowed our peahen friend a bit, and she and Bella appear to be a little more tolerant of each other. Bella doesn't fuss when Penelope comes on to the patio with the babies, and Penelope doesn't bait her — usually.

Bella has her freedom, and comes and goes as she pleases. Funny thing about that: now that I don't try to get her to come in, she usually turns up at the door just after it gets dark. She remains the consummate Zen master, and is a daily reminder of how to live: be yourself, love, and when you feel like it, take a nap.

As for we human characters, we're doing just fine.

For years Johann had been hoping for an opportunity to upgrade his Intermediate Paramedic qualification to the Advanced level. He'd remained committed to finding a good fulltime job that will enable him to make use of his skills and be rewarding both emotionally and financially. It hadn't seemed likely, however, because the bridge courses between Intermediate and Advanced had been done away with in the South African system. That meant that his decade-plus of experience in South Africa, South Sudan and Mozambique wouldn't count for anything; he'd have to start all over again and do a four-year university course which, of course, we couldn't afford.

He'd pretty much given up on the idea of getting the higher qualification, when — miraculously — he discovered a correspondence course he could do out of Australia. He's now finished the academic portion, with distinction, and will be doing the practical component later this year, likely at a clinic in Kenya.

This new qualification is accepted in one hundred and sixty countries. South Africa isn't one of them.

I still believe that things are always working out for me, even where the South African Department of Home Affairs is concerned, but eighteen months (and counting) later, I have yet to be granted Permanent Residence status.

While I wait, I'm still happily writing and creating art with Alicia as Two Girls and an Elephant. My volunteer work has expanded to include a grassroots organization called Nourish, where I help out with some exciting community projects, including supporting preschool education and women's microenterprises. I'm also helping to raise awareness for the Southern African Wildlife College. Both these not-for-profits are dedicated to conservation and poverty alleviation. I firmly believe the two go hand in hand, and that the only way to end the current poaching crisis is through the education and empowerment of the local communities.

Johann and I have many wonderful friends here, and we would love to stay in Hoedspruit. Maybe that's what will happen.

Or maybe not. If we do end up leaving, it will be without regrets, knowing that we've made the most of every day here, and taken advantage of every opportunity and experience that came our way. If it turns out that it's time to leave, we'll trust that it's life's way of moving us along and that it will ultimately be a good thing.

There may not always be elephants wherever life takes us, but I know one thing for sure: there'll always be miracles.

Acknowledgments

Thank you, Sarah Currie and Lynn Davis, for so graciously sharing your talents, your time and your insights. Above all else, thank you for all the years of fun and friendship we've shared, with so many more to come.

Thank you, Patricia Sands and Tony Park: your encouragement and guidance have helped me immeasurably as a writer. I'm paying it forward every chance I get! I value and appreciate your friendship.

Thanks, Tracey Hawthorne — it was a pleasure working with you again. Your suggestions were invaluable.

And thank you to family and friends on both sides of the world — Johann and I are lucky to have so many places where the door is always open and we feel at home.

About the author

In her native Canada, Jacquie Gauthier was a local radio and television personality, a playwright and producer, and for a short time, a politician. Her play *Jazzabel*, along with *Portraits*, the festival of one-woman shows she co-produced, was featured in Oprah Winfrey's *O Magazine*.

Since moving to South Africa in 2010 she continues to create her happily-ever-after with her beloved husband Johann. She's a writer, a certified nature guide, a teacher of English and adult literacy, an amateur photographer and an artistic entrepreneur. She's also the co-founder, with Alicia Fordyce, of Two Girls and an Elephant, a company combining photography, art and elephant conservation.

 www.twogirlsandanelephant.com

Made in the USA
San Bernardino, CA
15 February 2018